Memories
My Early Years in Germany and Sweden

Paul L. Kester

MEMORIES

My Early Years in Germany and Sweden

Paul L. Kester

Published by The Writer's Den
Buffalo, New York
2013

www.thekesters.net/memories

First Printing: 2013

ISBN: 978-1-304-53289-3

Published by The Writer's Den
Buffalo, New York
www.garyearlross.com

Photo Credits: All photos are from the author and his family, with the exception of the historical photos of Wiesbaden, which are from the collection of the Aktives Museum Spiegelgasse für Deutsch-Jüdische Geschichte in Wiesbaden

For Anya and Shiri with love

Introduction

Some twenty-five years ago, I started writing my memories. I was born in December 1925, and what began as a happy childhood with my family in Germany ended with my escape into Sweden on January 15, 1939.

Ten years later, in 1998, I continued my life's story, covering the years 1939 until the summer of 1942. I interrupted my story at the point of my coming to Stockholm, starting "adult" living, and dealing with the impact of the Holocaust on my life.

Now, at the age of 87, in early 2013, I continued the story and saw it through to its conclusion with my immigration to, and life in, the United States.

Going back and reading my diaries and letters, and looking again at many photos, I feel a deep sense of gratitude for the rich life I enjoyed. It was rich not in the sense of any material wealth accumulated, but rich in love and friendship.

I marvel at the enormous changes that I have witnessed during my lifetime. I remember the simple life of my childhood when pennies were a fortune, when horse-and-buggy provided transportation on the countryside, when flush toilets were a luxury, and when cars were

Paul Kester

only for the super-rich. Much has changed. Much was lost. Much was gained.

The three sections of my story were originally intended for my family. I wanted them to learn more about me, besides what is told in the Shoah Foundation interviews I gave on film in 1996, and in the other letters, documents and mementos in our possession or given to various museums.

Special thanks to my daughter-in-law Gunilla and my son Daniel for their suggestions and corrections, and for converting a stack of typewritten pages into a book with pictures.

Paul Kester

Part 1: Germany 1925-1939

To write down my memories seems difficult—it is easier to let my mind roam and recall events and incidents and to talk about them. To put them down on paper seems to be a formidable task. Not because some of it is painful. Not because some of it is difficult to remember. Not because my memory may be faulty. Rather, because it is difficult to describe the life of an era long gone. I envy the novelists who have the training to do this sort of thing. If world events had not shaped much of my early life, I might have acquired a greater facility to write more easily and to better express what I felt and experienced. But then I would have had much less to write about, and I would not have become fluent in three languages. I won't start out by saying "what if" but rather give it a try.

Earliest childhood memories

My sister Helen and I were lucky. We were not only our parents' only children, but also our maternal grandparents' only grandchildren. And we were the only children among the large Baum family in Wiesbaden and the Kleinstrass[*] families in Westfalen. Mother's cousins in Wiesbaden were too young to have children, and our Westfalen cousins were already grown up by the time we arrived. Of course, we accepted this huge family as the most normal thing in the world and the resulting benefits, e.g. presents, visits, and last but not least the

---

[*] Kleinstrass was Paul's family name. He changed it to Kester after coming to the U.S.

love and affection given to us. And there were the care and concern for us given by the *Kindermädchen* (nanny), the cleaning woman, household and store employees, neighbors, and friends. All this created a secure and often exciting childhood filled with small favors, surprises, special events, and fun activities. I was taught by my parents to say a nightly prayer:

> *"Lieber Gott, mach mich fromm*
> *Dass ich in den Himmel komm"*[*]

To this I regularly added more mundane requests that God should let the sun shine on Sunday so we could go to the *Strandbad*, and let there be snow so we could go sleigh riding. These two activities were of course not obtainable simultaneously, but either one appeared more desirable than going to heaven. The *Strandbad* was a beach resort on an island in the river Rhine. One went there by bus to the river and then by boat to the island. The boat trip for a three- or four-year-old was as exciting as several boat trips on much bigger boats later in life. I guess my earliest memory is being on one of these little boats and watching the pilot push the boat off the pier, a giant in command of the universe! I also remember walking on the river, when it froze during an exceptionally cold winter. Other early memories recall special annual events, e.g. the annual fair in November with its collection of merry-go-rounds, unique attractions, music, noises, foods, and smells.

---

[*] "Dear God, make me religious (devout), so that I will get into heaven."

Or Easter egg hunts, birthday parties, both our own or those of other children, and Mardi Gras with its fancy costumes and festivities. Or the visits to Westfalen, where Papa's relatives lived in small towns and villages, staying with favorite uncles and aunts, experiencing special foods, colorful festivals, picking fruit, admiring the animals. And we always had other children to play with, be it in Westfalen or at home in Wiesbaden.

At home the best day of the week was Sunday. First thing in the morning we wound up in Papa's bed. He told us stories from his childhood, when life was so much simpler and poorer. We indulged in

Paul and his sister Lena (Helen)

the knowledge that we had it so much better. And Papa predicted that when we grew up, there would be two Sundays every week. Imagine the unimaginable! Papa, the inveterate optimist, sure was right. The rest of Sunday, except for the *Strandbad* in summer and sleigh rides in winter, we spent by walking tours in the Taunus, a beautiful mountain area surrounding the town. We took along sandwiches for lunch, but in the afternoon we got cake and soft drinks in a country inn or café. Each season had its attraction: collect anemones in spring, chestnuts in fall, buy strawberries or plums or peaches from the farmers in the fields. Of course, this idyllic early childhood had its moments of frustrations and disappointments, such as childhood diseases, not getting a toy or a candy when wanting it badly, sibling jealousy, and all the other "Do's" and "Don'ts" any child has to suffer.

These early years took place in a time of economic and political upheaval. World War I had destroyed not Germany's cities (WWII would do that), but its spirit. When adults talked about normal times or the good old days, they meant the decades preceding 1914. Defeat in 1918, followed by a revolution, the breakdown of authority, and inflation had left deep scars. All this is history, and need not be retold by me. It did not intrude on the life of a boy four, five, or six years old. But I remember the beggars who would come to the door, usually around midmorning, asking for and receiving pennies or slices of bread. Or they would sing or play some barrel-organ or other instrument in the courtyard of our apartment building. I was allowed to wrap the penny in paper and throw it down. Or the collection of uni-

4

formed men assembling in a small square in our neighborhood listening to political speeches, or marching with their flags be they communist, socialist, rightist, or Nazi.

I remember the grinding poverty of the early thirties. The many signs of apartments for rent. The shabby clothing of the children who lived in primitive backyard apartments. The gulf that separated the poor people from us who were only lower middle class. At least, we maintained a lifestyle, if primitive by today's standards, which included simple but plenty of food, clean and well-kept living quarters, decent clothing, small luxuries for us children, books, concerts, thea-

Paul and Helen in the Taunus Mountains

ter, and eventually movies for the adults. A visit to a coffee house was routine, not only on Sundays. Otherwise, meals were always served at home and only for the family. Visitors, unless family or from out of town, came only for refreshments. The live-in maid was as much part of life as a refrigerator is in today's household. She was part of the family. When the last one, a young girl from a village in the Taunus, had to leave us in late 1935 because of the Nuremberg anti-Jewish legislation, she cried bitterly, and we children bade her a fond farewell.

The height of the depression in 1932, while not affecting us children, did not leave the family unscathed. Father's retail store of *Weisswaren* (linens, sheets, underwear) was closed down, and he went to work in Opa's[*] store. Opa's partner, his brother (Aunt Martha's husband), had died in 1930, so there was room or need for help. Besides, Papa's career as a window decorator came in handy, since Opa's store had lots of display windows. The grandparents gave up their large apartment and moved in with us, creating lots of togetherness and hectic discussions during mealtimes.

Opa was born 1869, one of six children. His oldest brother Albert was Lilo's (my cousin now in Paris) grandfather. The younger brother Moritz was Mike Kornberg's grandfather. The youngest brother Jacob died in Argentina, where he had joined his two daughters in 1937 or early 1938. One sister died in the twenties, the other, Mathilde, moved in with us in 1938, and stayed alive in Theresienstadt—until her final

---

[*] Opa = Grandfather

transport to Auschwitz in the summer of 1944. Opa was the most successful in the group, at least in terms of social standing in the com-community. After a business apprenticeship at the foremost jeweler in town (on completion of his employment he received the pocket watch still in our possession) he started with brother Moritz the firm *Gebrüder Baum*, a clothing store carrying high quality children's clothes, and ladies' lingerie, hose, and so on. The business was located in the *Kurviertel*, the elegant area around the best hotels, the theater and the *Kurhaus*, in the midst of expensive stores, and around the corner from Wilhelmstrasse, the famous boulevard of cafés and boutiques. The business benefitted from the *Kur* guests who visited the town for its health spa facilities. It was a successful business, especially before WWI. The after-effects of the war affected the business, but it en-

The family store, *Gebrüder Baum*, on the corner at the right, 1910

joyed a revival in the late twenties. It diminished in size during the depression of the early thirties, with a brief recovery during the early Nazi years until its destruction in 1938. Opa was one of Wiesbaden's more prominent citizens. He was a member of the city council, and also of the city school board. These were honorary positions, and they reflect his standing in the community. He had strong opinions and was outspoken. His love for and patience with his grandchildren was boundless. He helped with our homework. He took us to the circus. I don't know how he reacted to the Nazi era. The April 1, 1933 boycott of his store and all Jewish stores by the SA must have been a severe shock. He died in April 1935, six or eight weeks after being stricken

Opa: Siegfried Baum, Paul's grandfather

with cancer, two years after Hitler came to power.

Oma (grandmother), a widow at 59, was young by today's stand-ards, but seemed old to us. She worried about icy streets in wintertime, complained if we slammed doors during her rest period after the noon meal, and was a fussy eater claiming that certain foods did not agree with her. At times she appeared to be a demanding lady. She worked in the business all day, took part in charities, helped some poor people who lived on handouts, spoke French and English well, loved music and good books, and was a woman who was respected if not admired. She had travelled to New York in 1924 to visit her

Oma: Emilie Baum, Paul's grandmother

brother. She managed to get along with the many members of our extended family, and was treated with respect and affection by her contemporaries and very much by Mutti's generation. Every morning she would be in the store, handle the cash register, and more frequently serve the more distinguished customers who were pleased to be advised by Frau Baum. She had culture, charm, and a great sense of humor. She and I grew very close the last few years before my departure. She enjoyed my ability to write well, both poems and essays, to be receptive to music, to devour books both suitable and unsuitable for my age. She had lost both her parents very early in life, and had helped to raise several siblings. Her parents had been orthodox. She rejected the stricter forms of our religion, became quite assimilated, and had not been to a synagogue until the Hitler years, when it became a matter of loyalty to close ranks.

Papa was number four of seven children. The oldest were two sisters. One was cousin Micha's (now in Israel) grandmother, the other Werner's (another cousin in Israel) mother. Karl was the oldest brother and carried on the family business, a country store in Bredenborn. He never married, and the household was kept by the youngest sister, Frieda. Karl died of a heart attack in 1941, just in time to avoid deportation. Josef studied medicine, had a private practice in Hamm, and did not get married either. Hugo was a cattle dealer, who lived in Bredenborn. After he married a local girl, Änne, he built a new home in the early thirties where Hubert still lives. Hubert, Irmgard and Josef are their children, and the family survived thanks to Änne's being Catholic.

Papa finished grammar school at age 14, and started an apprenticeship in a nearby town as *Dekorateur*. He eventually worked in several cities until he got drafted in 1914. He briefly fought the Russians in the Baltic countries. He became seriously ill with "Ruhr" disease, a kind of dysentery, was hospitalized for a lengthy period, and eventually sent back to Germany. Unfit for further front line duty, he spent the remaining war years serving in a ground support unit for the fledgling German air force in Darmstadt near the French border.

In 1919 he resumed his career, and achieved quite a reputation. His window displays received favorable reviews in daily and trade

Abraham Kleinstrass,
Paul's grandfather

Albert Kleinstrass,
Paul's father

newspapers. He became chief decorator at Blumenthal, Wiesbaden's biggest department store. He was an ardent Skat player (a popular German card game), and belonged to the Jewish Skat Club. One of its members, Julius Kahn (his wife Emma was a first cousin of Oma) introduced him to "Hänschen," the name by which my mother was known among relatives and friends. They got engaged in 1921 and married in 1922. Lena (Helen) was born in 1923 and I in 1925.

Papa was a devoted family man and father. He was not young, born in 1883, and was in his early fifties during my school years. But he was flexible and active. He went to the store by bike instead of walking, which was quite unusual if not eccentric in those days. He taught us to swim and to ice skate, went sleigh riding with us, played games with us, and monitored closely our activities and progress. He was adamantly opposed to beating children, a very advanced approach for the times when a sound beating was considered a healthy ingredient in a child's upbringing. Our maids were specifically forbidden to touch us at the risk of getting fired. Erich Kornberg (Mike's father) much later quoted my father, *"Kinder schlägt man nicht"* as a shining example of modern education. Disobedience was punished by withholding special treats, e.g. sweets or dessert. Once or twice during my early school years I would not come home from school in time for the midday meal but explore with other boys the apple orchards in the area. The punishment was no meal, dry bread only. Such mortification was sufficient to discourage further unauthorized excursions. He emphasized and encouraged us to try our best to excel in school. Good test scores and report cards deserved financial rewards using the equivalent of the Richter scale: 2 (Good) was worth 10 Pfennig, a 1 (Excellent) was worth one Mark. And we were taught to be thrifty. Our weekly allowance, starting with a few pennies during the early school days eventually, I believe, reached one Mark during my *Gymnasium* (high school) days. The awards for good school performance helped to augment these funds, since we had to pay for school supplies (nothing was free, not books and not paper, pencils, or pens) and, of course, for the much desired candies and ice cream. When we started religious school, aged six or seven, and learned about Jewish customs and traditions, Papa started making a Seder (using a modern Haggadah), blessed us on Friday nights, joined us in saying the *brochoth* and read with us the *Tischgebet* saying grace after dinner. He delighted to surprise us, finding Easter eggs in the forest, kidding us on April Fools' Day, preparing birthday gifts, and challenging us to compete with him in various sport activities. I was 12 when I finally managed to run a faster 100 meters than he did.

Mutti, my mother, was well educated. She went to the *Lyceum* (girls' high school) with Alice Keiles, her classmate and best friend during school days and for life. In 1913 or early 1914 (she was born 1897), she went to England. I don't recall if she stayed with a family or in a boarding school. She had to return hastily in August 1914 so she would not get stuck in England as an enemy alien. Opa met her on her return in Holland (neutral ground). She spoke English and French. French was more in demand in Wiesbaden, it being the primary international language until WWII. Mutti worked in the family business, doing the record and bookkeeping. I don't know if she had studied this after high school, but I think she spent some time in a girls' boarding school where young ladies from establishment families were trained for whatever role they were expected to perform later in life.

Mutti was less patient with us than Papa. She had to cope with all the details of daily life, and didn't mind telling us, or yelling at us, to reach results. She was popular among the many relatives and friends. Everybody was fond of Hänschen as she was called by those who were on a first name basis with her. She exuded goodness and friendliness. Both parents were positive individuals, industrious, helpful, and cheerful. They enjoyed family life. They had a large circle of

Wedding of Paul's parents, 1921

friends for Skat, bridge, and social get-togethers. There were no fights in the family. Only once was Mutti upset when Papa did not want to join some family festivity (I don't remember why he did not want to attend), but eventually Papa did go, and love and harmony were restored. This incident sticks in my mind, because disagreement between our parents just did not happen. Still today I find it painful to encounter family arguments among others, be they friends or strangers, having been exposed in my childhood only to affection and tolerance among large family groups. Aunt Martha later would comment that in spite of different personalities, lifestyles, resources, and opinions there were no fights between any of the brothers, sisters, and their spouses. Only when Martha and her sister Berthel in their high

Johanna and Albert Kleinstrass, Paul's parents

eighties had to share a small apartment, did they argue and criticize each other, but they managed to stay together.

We were exposed early to books. The German fairy tales and children's books were scary. The *Struwwelpeter* with the tailor and his huge scissors who cuts off the fingers of children who suck their thumb was enough to make me fearful since I did not suck just one thumb but all of two fingers. And the *Suppenkasper*, who dies of star-vation for not eating his soup, and the kid who cannot sit quietly at the dinner table and gets buried under the tablecloth with all the dishes. Life had its risks and I learned to be careful! And Grimm's fairy tales were grim. I must have had a lively imagination because I could sit still in the morning in a corner in our apartment, while the maid cleaned up around me and enjoy an imaginary train ride to *Himpfen*, a non-existing town. My love for train rides and boat trips started early, and I still enjoy them today. I could easily occupy myself without or-ganized supervision, and did not go to a Kindergarten, except in Bredenborn where I disliked it thoroughly and did not have to go after a while. Otherwise, Westfalen was heaven on earth and the high point of every summer, and other seasons.

The start of school in the spring of 1932 was a major event: excit-ing, exhilarating, traumatic. Exciting because of its newness, starting with the *Schultüte* (a fancy carton filled with sweets), and walking to and from school (after a few guided tours with Mutti) alone, and the new impressions, friends, surroundings, and learning. We had the same teacher for all subjects for all of the four years of elementary school. She became a person of major influence and authority in my life. Her name was Fraulein Hief. She could be warm and caring, and then again mean and screaming. The way she beat up little boys can only be considered psychotic, but maybe that was the accepted way of raising children. Minor offenses were punished by getting hit hard on one's fingers with a thin bamboo stick. Major punishment was inflicted by bending down and having one's behind whipped mercilessly. This indignity I suffered only once when I had not done some homework. I had forgotten the assignment or had not gotten around to doing it. Being a bright and diligent student made my school days quite pleasant, and what some of my fellow classmates had to suffer seemed quite normal and ordinary. The school was located in a district where roughly half the children came from middle class families, and the other half from a poor neighborhood. I walked to and from school through part of the poorer district, and I can still see the Communist and Socialist flags in the windows of those miserable apartments, but of course only until the Nazis came to power in 1933.

I always took two sandwiches along for our 10 o'clock rest period (breakfast was minimal, one roll and a cup of cocoa), one for me and one for the big basket from which the poor children received theirs. The walk to and from school took probably not much more than ten minutes, but seemed quite lengthy. In spite of political upheaval and a normal level of crime, poverty, and misery, there was never any fear or risk for the safety of children. We played in the streets and walked the city without trepidation. A neighbor's boy joined me in these walks. He was quite dominating and not very bright, and probably jealous of me for coming from a more well-to-do

Paul, Paul and Helen, Paul and Helen, Paul's first day of school

home and doing well in school. I disliked him and his irrational behavior, but was admonished to keep his company. Eventually, he moved away, and I enjoyed my walks more fully in the company of children of my choice. I became friendly with Leo Kahn, who lived around the corner from us. He was in the same school and grade level, even though in another class. But we were in the same religious class and Jewish sport club, and became classmates in the *Gymnasium* and inseparable. We shared school and most other activities until we both left Germany, headed for different countries and destinies.

Memories from grammar school 1932 to 1936 are fragmented yet vivid. I could easily cope with the scholastic requirements and had no problem with the social adjustment. I soon learned to read and became a voracious consumer of printed material—newspapers, magazines, and books. Books for children, funny stories, sad stories, boys' books, girls' books, books from my parents' library both those approved and those identified as not for children. Collecting stamps also became a passion, which I shared with Leo.

I was seven years old when Hitler came to power. The pictures of Hitler and his gang were everywhere. Immediately after he took over, we were inundated by a massive propaganda effort. I remember the torch parades, the martial music, and the flags. In March 1933, we all marched from school to one of the city's major assembly halls to listen to the radio transmission of the opening of the *Reichstag* at Potsdam, (the parliament building having burnt down a few weeks earlier) where the old president Hindenburg let Hitler officially assume his new leadership role. May 1 became a Nazi labor festival day with flags and green branches and flowers in every window and balcony. We had the flowers, but I missed the flags on our balcony. The celebrations and demonstrations in support of the new regime were impressive, certainly for a seven-year-old. The old Roman edict "give the people bread and circus" was diligently followed, circus right away and bread more slowly. But through the building of huge public works, by militarizing the population, and by rearming, a level of prosperity was created which provided security and pride for the masses. There were few opponents. Those who could not stomach the

The Kleinstrass family: Paul, Albert, Helen, and Johanna

new regime either left the country, or made themselves invisible, or shut up.

The first openly anti-Semitic event took place on April 1, 1933, when the S.A. marched in front of Jewish stores, intimidating potential customers to enter. The elimination of Jews from the professions and public service followed. All this is history. Emigration started. My cousin Albert Rosenbaum (Micha's father), left for Palestine. He had worked at Blumenthal, the department store, had witnessed the April 1 boycott and decided it was time to leave. Another cousin, Werner Rothenberg, was kicked out from the university where he had started to study dentistry. He went to Palestine in 1934. As for Eugene Hervey's parents, the mother was Russian born and much more apprehensive towards state-sponsored anti-Semitism. They were vacationing in Switzerland in January 1933, and the mother refused to return to Germany, so they never came back. Only a small minority was that flexible, or had the resources and knowhow to start a new life in a foreign country. Most could not pack up and go, leave the country where for generations they had been accepted as citizens, where their ancestors had lived for hundreds of years, and where emancipation and assimilation had progressed rapidly during the decades following the Napoleonic wars. Emotional ties to family and friends and to the country of their birth, its language and culture, provided identity and a sense of belonging. One could not abandon all this because of anti-Semitic policies of a government which was not given much of a chance to last. Last but not least who could walk away from his business, his livelihood, his possessions, and elderly parents, only to expose himself and his children to a beggar's exist-ence in a foreign country where he was not needed or wanted?

The early years 1933 to 1936 were fun years for us children. There was no anti-Semitism among classmates or teachers at school, and there was an active social life for us children in the Jewish com-munity. Religious education in the afternoon, sport activities at the Jewish sport club, attending services on Friday night and on holidays, club activities Saturday afternoon—all provided enjoyment and stimulation. Of course, we were aware of our special status, and we learned quickly what to say and not to say, depending on whom we talked to. I saw the April boycott, and sensed the impact it had on the adults. The Nuremberg laws in 1935 were shocking and upsetting. Jews lost their civil rights. We could no longer have gentile household help under the age of 45, and a long list of other restrictions and pro-hibitions were passed. We children assumed some household chores. I polished all the shoes, and cleaned the kitchen once a week. Other tasks, both in the home and running errands, added to a busy and ac-tive life! We knew that some people were Nazis, that others were friendly, and again others were if not friendly at least ambivalent. In the apartment house where we lived, we knew the friendly people and also the others. The only family with children our age, moved in dur-ing the Nazi era. The father had some official position, which demanded non-fraternization. This caused a distinct separation and avoidance of each other, which was well understood by them and us. But there was no open hostility.

I was fascinated by *Der Stürmer*, an anti-Semitic weekly newspaper, which one could read in display cases put up all over town, so the public could read it free of charge. The ugly cartoons of Jews, the gory stories, the nefarious drivel had to be seen and read to believe that this was happening in the *Land der Denker und Dichter* (land of thinkers and poets). Then there was the excitement when the Saar district in early 1935 rejoined the Fatherland, when shortly thereafter the military draft was initiated, when the Versailles treaty was repudiated, when the Rhineland in 1936 was militarized. These events, in addition to the regular Nazi festival days, the constant marches, parades, endless speeches, celebrations, exhortations at school and in the streets were exciting for a young boy, in spite of his distinct awareness that he was not part of them. How the times affected the grownups can

In the Rhine wine district, 1932.
Albert and Johanna with the Loeb, Meyer and Katz families

only be imagined. When getting to the store in the morning, my grandmother would always exchange greetings with her neighbor, whose husband owned a kitchen supply and appliance store across the street from our store. After 1933, this woman stopped greeting Oma. Such indignities were annoying, and what added to make life miserable was the uncertainty of not knowing what this government would do next to make life more burdensome. WWI, postwar upheaval, inflation, depression, and political strife had conditioned people to hardship and deprivations. But to be rejected, resented, and restricted by government decree only for belonging to a religious minority was a heavy emotional burden for people who had been so much a part of society for so long.

In early 1935, Opa was ailing. Doctors came to the house. X-rays were studied. After a while he was hospitalized, where we visited him—the last time in early April. By that time he was visibly suffering excruciating pain and could barely enjoy seeing us. A few days later he died. Death was a new experience, awesome, but interesting. The formalities, black wardrobe, black-bordered announcements, condolence letters and cards, many visitors to the house, *Kaddish* in the evening—all was strange and fascinating. Oma and my parents did not display their grief in any demonstrative manner. The event was not unexpected, and they made every effort to face the inevitable with their usual dignity. When later that year the Nazis passed the Nuremberg laws, I remember Oma's reaction: she was glad that Opa did not live to be faced with this event as the insult of this legislation would have been a devastating blow to him.

In the spring of 1936 I was ten years old and was finishing the first four years of grammar school. To get enrolled in a *Gymnasium* was the next step towards a higher education. This required certain scholastic achievements including passing official exams, all of which I could handle with ease. I had developed a facility to express myself well in writing, and I excelled in writing essays and compositions. My parents and Oma were often wryly amused reading my vivid descriptions of the bad Communists in Russia and the heroic deeds of German emperors and other heroes. I don't recall any essays in praise of Hitler and his cohorts, but I probably glorified the admirable German nation and its claim to greatness. However, I grew up with the knowledge that Nazism was bad for us Jews, and that we eventually

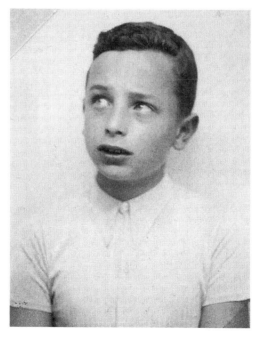

Paul

would have to emigrate. I learned to cope with the concept of "Them" and "Us," how to behave or what to say or NOT to say, depending on who was listening. Children adapt easily. What is absurd and danger-ous to adults can seem perfectly normal to children, because they don't know the difference. We adjusted to new experiences all the time, never mind if times were normal or abnormal. And the family, while making us aware of who we were and why, made every effort to keep life normal for us, and not to burden us children with all their concerns and anxieties.

My father proceeded to take the necessary steps to get me into a *Gymnasium*. Because he was a WWI veteran, he was entitled to enroll us in a high school. The one closest to home was the obvious choice. However, the principal of this institution informed my father that he and the faculty all were strong supporters of Nazism. He would not assure the safety of a Jewish child in his school. The second *Gymna-sium* declined my application with a less blunt excuse. The third and last (*Gutenbergschule*)—there were only three *Gymnasium* in town— accepted me and also my friend Leo. In retrospect, one could question Papa's insistence to get me into one of these schools. There were Jew-ish schools in Mainz (a longer commute) and later also in Wiesbaden. But he felt strongly the need to get us into the best educational pro-gram, and was not willing to give up what legal rights he still had. I am glad he did it. The training I enjoyed during the ensuing two and a half years was excellent. I learned how to study, how to absorb knowledge quickly, how to cope with a variety of teachers (one for each subject) and to compete with bright boys from all over the city.

In grammar school, I was one of a few good students. At the *Gymnasium* they were all good, since the entrance exams weeded out the less gifted ones. In class, we sat two students sharing a set of seats and desks. First I shared it with another boy, a friendly fellow, who incidentally for whatever reason was one of very few boys who was not a member of the Hitler Youth. Later, Leo Kahn and I sat together pursuant to some school or government ruling to protect Hitler's boys from unnecessary contact with us. While the Nazi indoctrination accelerated rapidly during my *Gymnasium* years, Leo and I experienced no hostility from our teachers. They treated us like all other boys; they were demanding and strict. We were good students, and the teachers, many of whom were party members, accepted us on our merits. Occasionally, a few of the boys called us bad names or made us feel uncomfortable, but this was not often. Considering the volume of anti-Jewish propaganda that they were exposed to in the press, radio, and the Hitler Youth, they were not hostile and pretty decent kids. My Aryan looks and Leo's attractive dark eyes, red cheeks, and dark hair did not fit the *Stürmer* pictures of Jews. Our appearance did not single us out which helped us to be accepted.

In one class, it was Biology or Geography, we learned about the different races. One lecture covered the Jewish race with pictures and charts displaying the inferior features of Jews and the superior bodies and faces of the Nordic Aryans. Now this was Wiesbaden, a spa town already mentioned in Roman literature, where legions from all directions had marched through or settled throughout thousands of years, and where the faces of the boys in the class reflected the multitude and mixture of tribes that had populated the Rhineland over the centuries. Very few, if any, in the class personified the Nordic superman. The teacher concluded his informative lecture by explaining the fact that the two Jewish boys in this class did not look like the stereotypes on the blackboard, was because this was only a lecture in theory which did not always coincide with reality. And he also admonished the class not to use the lecture as an excuse to be nasty to Leo and me.

In the beginning, we participated in the recurring assemblies because of national celebrations or semester starts or endings, which always included the singing of the national anthems (the Horst Wessel song, and the *Deutschland Über Alles* song) where we did the Hitler salute with raised right arm. Later, Leo and I were excused from these

English class, 1937: Paul's best friend, Leo Kahn, is at the far right

exercises. Also, during those years, the Hitler salute became the standard greeting at the beginning and end of every lecture (we had five or six lectures each day). I don't remember if we eventually were excused also from participating in this custom.

The curriculum put great emphasis on sports. We had five sub- jects: gymnastics, swimming, track and field, games, and one I have forgotten. All required passing grades to get promoted to the next class. I did well in these categories too, partly thanks to extensive training over the years at the Jewish sport club.

Friends and relatives leave Germany in more frequent numbers. The Jakob Baums join their daughters in Paraguay. The Loeb family (Laura Zeisel) leaves for New York. Aunt Martha to the USA. Others go to North or South America or Palestine or South Africa. Our par- ents try to get us on a children's program to the U.S., but it does not materialize. Talk about emigration becomes more dominant. Then, in 1938, Oma's brother in New York agrees to send an affidavit for one of us children. Helen, the older one, is the one to go. In late May, she travels with Papa to Stuttgart to get her visa at the American consu- late. In early June is her confirmation, when all 14-year-old girls in a solemn and festive ceremony in the synagogue are consecrated in the Jewish faith. It is a memorable event even though we cannot imagine that it is going to be one of the last happy ceremonies in our syna- gogue. After services, friends and relatives visit us to congratulate. The many gifts make me look forward to my Bar Mitzvah later this year. In the evening there is a big dinner party at home, the last family get-together of its kind. Aunt Frieda is there from Bredenborn, Änne Kahn from Strasbourg, her parents, the Kornbergs from Essen, the Julius Kahn's, and Liesel Stamm, Oma's niece (the antique chest, the book press, and the Daumier print we have come from her belongings. She spent the war years in England, and lived thereafter in Israel). A few days later, Helen visits the relatives in Essen and Westfalen to say good-bye, and on June 28 she leaves Wiesbaden with Mutti who accompanies her to Hamburg to see her off.

My calendar for 1938 reflects very normal activities. The major events dealt with the acquisition of roller skates in late spring, getting Uncle Josef's bike in May, and thereafter being allowed to use it for

Helen's confirmation, June, 1938

commuting to and from school. And the excursions on Sundays in the Taunus, and during the week a full schedule with violin lessons, sport activities, religious school, private English lessons, attending services on Friday nights, spending Saturday afternoons with Leo and Lothar, another friend, going to the movies or playing. Also helping out at the store on free days and afternoons delivering packages to customers, or running errands to the post office or similar jobs, activities that earned me extra pocket money. A few days after Helen's departure, summer vacation starts, and I am off for one more glorious stay in Westfalen. First I visit the Kornbergs in Essen, then Uncle Josef in Hamm, and then the usual happy time in Brakel and Bredenborn. Back in Wiesbaden by mid-August, life continues with all customary activities plus special lessons to prepare for my Bar Mitzvah scheduled for December 31. For the first time, I fast all day on Yom Kippur and spend all morning and late afternoon at the synagogue. Only in the afternoon, am I together with Leo and Lothar. In September, there is much excitement about the Sudetenland, and talk of war. By October first "peace in our time" has been secured by the British and French, and Hitler has prevailed.

Life goes on. Leo, Lothar and I enjoy our Saturday afternoons, organize children's birthday parties and theater plays, and go to the movies. In late October we enjoy the annual *Kirmes*. Early November continues as normal. I continue to help in the store, although it is to be shut down in a few months after a sale of the existing merchandise during the forthcoming Christmas season. The slow decline of non-Jewish customers and the ongoing plans for emigration to America, hopefully during the following year, plus increasingly restrictive regulations for Jewish businesses make it impossible to keep the store.

On November 10, Leo and I are in school. During the mid-morning recess, the school administrator tells Leo and me to go home—the synagogue is burning and there is trouble. We go home. Mutti and Oma are at home, upset. Dad is in hiding with Julius Katz.

When Mutti and Oma walked to the store, they saw the synagogue in flames, and the store smashed to pieces. Dad had arrived earlier in the morning at the store to open up. There was a huge crowd

The Michaelsberg Synagogue, Wiesbaden.
Kristallnacht, November 9-10, 1938

in front of the store, watching or participating in its destruction. Dad was asked by two police officials to come with them. As the three of them tried to push through the crowd, the one in front of Dad told Dad to slow down. The police in back told Dad to speed up. So Dad speeded up, made a sideway move and disappeared. Somehow he met Julius Katz. They learned that all Jewish men were being rounded up. So they gathered some clothes and food, and spent the next few days in hiding in the Taunus. First, they thought they might escape to France, the nearest border, but the borders were even more closely watched than before. And the use of trains was an invitation to immediate arrest.

Somehow, the day comes to a close, the despair of the grown-ups palpable, as the news gets worse and more frightful. It is decided that Leo and I go back to school on Friday. The school day passes peacefully. Our math teacher, an elderly man, allows himself a comment that the prior day's destruction was not meaningful. On Saturday, a normal school day, we are asked to the principal's office and told that new government regulations no longer allow our presence at school. Leo and I go home. Twelve-year-olds adjust quickly to sudden events, and an unexpected vacation is a tolerable development. Sunday I spend with Lothar and Leo. Monday I start working in the store, cleaning up the indescribable mess. As the legal owner of the store, Oma declares bankruptcy. The destruction of fixtures and merchandise, and the requirement that the owners have to pay for the cleanup and repair of their destroyed or damaged property do not allow for payment of creditors whose claims would have been covered during the planned orderly closing of the store.

Monday it appears that the arrests of Jewish men have come to an end. Papa comes back on Tuesday. Tuesday evening, it is past 8 p.m., the doorbell rings. I open the door. A man in civilian clothes, middle-aged, identifies himself as Gestapo and asks for my father. Papa is told to pack a small suitcase, and off he goes with this official who handled the arrest without hostility but in a matter-of-fact manner, like it's all in a day's or night's work. Within minutes, Papa is gone. Mutti sends me immediately on my bike to the Katz family, to warn Mr. Katz. He and his wife are already in bed, presumably with a stomach flu. If I recall correctly, he was not picked up because of his illness. I ride back home, on this dismal rainy November night. Next day, I go with Mutti to police headquarters. We are not admitted, nor given any information about Papa's whereabouts. The next two weeks, I work in the store, collecting the mass of broken glass and sorting out the damaged partitions, pieces of furniture, display racks, and other items. With more than ten big window displays and dozens of display cases, the store was a sea of glass fragments and splintered wood. Everything was smashed. I don't recall if there was any looting. Probably not, since the destruction took place under the supervision and participation of the SA, the Nazi party militia. Much of the glass breakage had been accomplished by throwing manikins, or broken parts of manikins—heads, arms, and legs—like soccer balls against the glass structures.

Two weeks of cleanup and the depressing atmosphere at home are unforgettable. I would wake up at night with the noise of the broken glass, which during the day I would scoop up for hours on end, ringing in my ears. I can only imagine the turmoil that Oma and Mutti have gone through. Mutti tries to maintain some level of normalcy. I continue English lessons, and after two weeks when the store was finally turned over to the receiver, I start working for Arthur Strauss, the administrator of the Jewish Community and a close family friend. In the meantime, the news of what has happened elsewhere, hits us all.

I believe we found out that Papa was in Dachau. We may have received a card from him or were told by the police. We learned that Uncle Karl and cousin Ernst were in Buchenwald, Uncle Josef in

The family store boarded up after Kristallnacht

Sachsenhausen. Most men from Wiesbaden were in either Buchen-wald or Dachau, concentration camps that would gain much greater notoriety at the end of WWII. On November 21, we got the news that Ernst, age 27, had died in Buchenwald. Two days later Aunt Emma, Oma's beloved cousin in Wiesbaden, learned that her husband, Julius Kahn, died at Buchenwald, and a few days later that her brother, Leo Baer, died. He was the father of one of my childhood friends, Hans Georg. These men somehow did not withstand the concentration camp treatment or for whatever reason were singled out by their guards and beaten to death. Oma and Mutti had to cope with these events, in addition to the bankruptcy with its complex arrangements, with Papa in the KZ (concentration camp) with so many others, and no assurance who would return alive and when.

I remember the inquiries: where are the men? What does it take to get them released? At this time, several European countries declare their willingness to save Jewish children, the *Kindertransport*. Mutti gets me on a list for Holland. Leo is already on this list; he has rela-tives in Amsterdam. A letter from Änne in Strasbourg (Lilo's mother) arrives. They try to get me out to France. Mutti also puts me on a list to England. England took in 10,000 children, the largest rescue effort at that time.

On December 7 Leo leaves, and I see him off at the Wiesbaden railway station. Finally, a letter arrives from Hedi, a distant relative, in Sweden. She put me on a list for Västraby, a Jewish boarding school for refugee children, where she and her husband are teachers.

Sweden is accepting several hundred children, and Västraby is to take 40 of them. Shortly thereafter, this letter is followed by a letter from the Swedish consulate in Berlin stating that my visa is available.

I continue working for Strauss. In between I go occasionally to the train station whenever men are expected back from the KZs. I see some of them come back—emaciated, dirty. Then, one midmorning while at the Strauss office, I get the message—Papa is back home. I rush home, wondering and worrying about his appearance and condition. He looks well; by the time I come home he wears clean clothes, and is his usual positive self. His good physical condition helped him to cope and to withstand all hardships. Also, somehow he became friendly with the camp barber who managed occasionally to help Dad to avoid some of the daily endless *Appells* where the men had to stand for many hours at attention in the open cold, raw, and rainy November air. His ability to manage adversity and his undiminished optimism helped him to overcome this experience without apparent physical or mental damage.

On December 14, my 13th birthday, I start the Jewish school, but I stay only until December 21 when winter vacation starts. I get the choice of having my Bar Mitzvah on the original date, December 31, in a temporary prayer hall in Wiesbaden, or at a later date in Västraby. I choose the Swedish alternative, as the event in Wiesbaden would be too dismal and disappointing. On December 23, Papa and I take the train to Brakel. We stay at the Rothenbergs and next day we go by bus to Bredenborn. I remember the evening December 24. It has been snowing. It is cold. Clear. Snow is on the ground and on the roofs and trees, the sky is starlit. The village is quiet, peaceful. I walk to the baker to pick up bread. It all looks like a Christmas card—idyllic—a perfect world. Except our lives are in turmoil! Uncle Karl is back from Buchenwald, where he saw Ernst beaten to death—it was not the only incident of its kind. Uncle Josef is there, back from Sachsenhausen. The talk is sad. The store in Bredenborn is closed and in liquidation. The enormous special tax assessment on Jewish property and assets wipes out whatever Jewish wealth remains. For those who manage to leave the country, there is an additional departure tax (*Reichsfluchtsteuer*). The future is uncertain: how to get out fast? Where to go? It is the beginning of the end for the Jews of Europe.

A couple of days later, I give a hug and a kiss to all. It is goodbye to Westfalen, the vacation paradise of my childhood. It is goodbye to Papa's family. Their love for us was so real, and their understanding and patience for us children complete. I will return eight and a half years later—the village unchanged—the family long gone. *Haus Kleinstrass* is no more. By then, it has become a home for German refugees from the Eastern provinces. Eventually, it is sold and torn down, to be replaced by some modern structure. A late evening and night trip by train back to Wiesbaden, so Papa can meet his weekly appearance at the Gestapo headquarters—the latest requirement invented as further harassment. A few more days in Wiesbaden, December 29 to January 9, packing, shopping. Last minute formalities. I accompany Papa for his weekly visit to the Gestapo. He and I go to the Hitler Youth headquarter to obtain a certificate that I am not a member, supposedly a requirement of the Swedish authorities. Lots of visitors, the men reminiscing (Papa, Erich Kornberg—Mike's father, Hans Keiles—Alice's husband, and others) of their four weeks in Dachau. The talk is about quota numbers, visas, affidavits—what to do, where to go. Last minute goodbye visits, presents, farewells.

Early January 9, it's off to the station. Oma says goodbye in the hallway, calm and smiling. Her last words: a blessing. Aunt Matilde (Opa's sister) is her usual tearful self. Mutti, Papa, and I take the bus to the station. Mutti and I say goodbye at the train station, a few words of good wishes and hope for an early reunion. Papa comes with

The Kleinstrass house in Bredenborn

me to Frankfurt where I have to catch the train to Berlin. The train is waiting. I secure a seat, Papa walks along the train, it's goodbye. I feel relief—finally I am off. The huge Frankfurt train station disappears, and the trip goes fast. The train passes through Weimar: the city of Goethe, the Weimar Republic, and Buchenwald personifies the contradictions inherent in German history and behavior. Will the train pass close by the KZ? I look for this place of the recent outrage, but don't see it. The train stops at Leipzig. The train station—the biggest in Germany—attracts my attention. Arrival in Berlin: Grete (Werner's sister) and her husband Georg pick me up. I stay at the apartment of Georg's aunts whom I have met before during vacation trips to Brakel. They have a large apartment near Kurfürstendamm.

Next morning we go to the Swedish consulate. The official takes one look at my *Kinderausweis*. He cannot give me the visa because my document does not have the J (for *Jude* or Jew) on it. We send the document back to Wiesbaden by express mail. By Thursday, two days later, I have my *Ausweis* back with a big red J stamped on it, and the visa is issued. The mail surely functioned well in those days. The lack of a J in my travel document was caused by the following incident: when it first became known that children were accepted by the various European countries, it was also announced that we did not need formal German passports, but that a *Kinderausweis* (child's identity card) would suffice. This was a much less complex procedure, and more quickly obtainable from the German authorities. Mutti and I went to police headquarters to get this document (this was during the time Papa was at Dachau).

We wait—I don't remember how long—in the shabby waiting hall with others in a similar predicament, which makes it a less than cheerful exercise. Eventually, we get admitted to the right official. *"And what do you want?"* We state our request. *"Name?" "Fathers name?" "Mother's maiden name?"* We provide the answers. When Mutti answers the last question with *"Baum,"* the snotty official suddenly smiles and asks: *"Are you the sister of Walter Baum?" "No, I am his cousin."* Whereupon a lively conversation ensues, the subject being the whereabouts of Walter (living in the USA since the 1920s), who had been a classmate of the official. In no time I get the document, and as a gesture of goodwill he leaves off the J, which was mandatory for all documents and passports.

I enjoy the days in Berlin, its sights and sounds. Sunday morning Georg takes me to the Stettiner Bahnhof, the Berlin train station for trains to Sweden. Off it goes through the flat lands of northern Germany. We had been unable to find out if, as a child, I was allowed to have 10 Marks on me which was all adult Jews could take with them when they left Germany. To play it safe I eat in the *Speisewagen* and buy two boxes of chocolates for my remaining funds, reducing my ready cash to 10 Pfennig. Near Sassnitz, the border station, the *Grenzpolizei*, a branch of the SS, comes to my compartment. I have a tiny suitcase. My luggage had been sent ahead after thorough inspection by the authorities that I would not take out of Germany anything of value other than my clothes and personal belongings. The contents of my little suitcase get inspected. A book, *The History of the German Jews*, a last minute farewell gift is taken by the official. He has to find out if I am allowed to take it out. After a while he comes back and tells me it is *Verboten*, and therefore confiscated. I could not care less. We approach the Baltic Sea, and the train goes on the ferry. I see an ocean for the first time. It is foggy, wet, and quiet. The boat takes off. I worry about seasickness, but the trip (a few hours) is uneventful. I walk outside on deck in the cold January night. I am elated. I got out. I am free. I feel a tremendous relief. The misery of the last two months is behind me. Whatever happens now can only be better. We get to Trelleborg, a town in southern Sweden.

I am in Sweden, a country nobody in Wiesbaden knew much about except that it was somewhere far away in the cold North. A

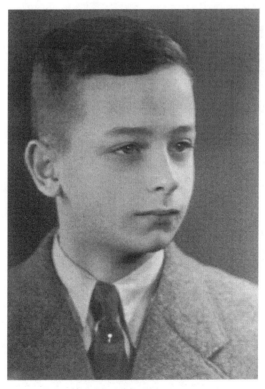

Paul, December, 1938

country that not only gave me refuge, but that eventually enchanted me with its beauty, and enriched my life beyond what I could possibly imagine on this dark winter day. I am very conscious that I am no longer on German soil but in a country where it is not a crime to be Jewish. I know this is a most important event in my life. But I cannot suspect that I will never see my family again or that my arrival in Sweden will have assured my survival.

The train from Trelleborg moves north. I wonder what RÖKNING FÖRBJUDEN means, but assume that it is not a sign spelling out special restrictions for Jews, as it includes the German word "*Jude*." The conductor indicates to me to get ready as we arrive in Eslöv. I get off the train. It must be 9 o'clock at night. Hedi and another teacher meet me. A quick car ride to Västraby. Hedi shows me to my room. I sleep in an upper bunk bed. Hedi warns me that some of the boys in the room might want to play tricks on me. But everybody is friendly. They only want to know—did I bring any *Schmonzes* (candies)?

PART 2:

January 1939 – September 1942

(written in 1998)

Ten years in Sweden—in retrospect it was survival in paradise. To call it paradise might be naive considering the days, and weeks, and even months of rain and sleet, the hardships and deprivations—both physical and emotional—the regimentation by harassed teachers and narrow-minded civil servants—all this and so much more will hardly resemble an imaginary life in heaven. But to live in peace and acceptable comfort in Europe during the first half of the forties, to be young and alive, to experience the challenges and pleasures of youth, to develop a keen appreciation for music and literature, to make friends for life, to enjoy the unique beauty of the Swedish countryside and of Stockholm on lovely summer days—all this and so much more was certainly paradise. If 55 years later I remember those days through rose-colored glasses, if I look back with nostalgia, so be it. It was a time when the world around us suffered utter destruction, when millions fought and killed and starved and died. We lived at the edge of this catastrophe, knowing what went on, yet preoccupied with the worries and pleasures of daily life. This need to cope with daily living plus the young people's single-minded capacity to pursue their own objectives and to overcome misfortune helped to make those years a time of growth and excitement. Let me try to remember, let me try to tell it. *I will use italicized text when quoting diaries or notes I kept and letters I received during those years.*

I am taking on this task at the suggestion and request of my daughter-in-law Gunilla, seconded by my son Daniel. To give them insight into our lives, and to pass on to Anya and Shiri a story for them to learn about their Mamama and Papapa in future years when we only live in their memories. It is not a unique story. It is the story of children growing up in Europe during unusual times, a lucky story. We were not very special. We were what is now called "good kids" who took advantage of the opportunities that were given to us.

VÄSTRABY

On a damp and chilly winter day, January 15, 1939 I arrived at Västraby, a boarding school 2 km from the village of Löberöd, 20 km from Lund, the nearest town. A distant relative (Aunt Martha's niece) Hedi Wolf and her husband Ernst were teachers at this school. When the school was allotted a couple of dozen or so of the 500 or 600 children to be taken in by Sweden from Nazi Germany through the *Kindertransport*, Hedi managed to get me on the list for this school. Here I was, just one month past my 13th birthday and two months after the November pogroms against us Jews in Germany, known as "*Kristallnacht*," for the first time in a foreign country and for the first time in boarding school. I had never been to a *Kinderheim* before, since vacations were always spent in Bredenborn, the village in Westphalia where my father had been born and members of his family still lived. But I felt comfortable from the first moment. I had learned to adjust to adverse conditions during the years when I attended the Nazi school in Wiesbaden. So this new experience was easy by comparison. Also, my natural ability to get along with people helped me then, as it did throughout my life, to quickly fit in and enjoy life in these new surroundings.

I stayed in a room with six or seven other boys, ages 9 to 15. Two of the boys were Georg Herzfeld and Herb Leitner, both from Vienna, who arrived on January 16, 1939, the day after I did. After a few weeks, the three of us were moved to another room where we were eight boys, ages 11 to 14. Besides Georg and Herb, there was Fredi Hahn, the youngest in the room. We were on the ground floor, close to the classrooms. The days started at some ungodly hour (it seemed that way at least in winter) with a half hour of exercising in the hall,

Västraby

followed by quickly getting washed and dressed. Then there was an assembly, I guess to make sure that all children were accounted for, to sing a happy birthday song for the one(s) who happened to have a birthday, and for whatever announcements the teacher-in-charge considered significant. This early get-together was followed by breakfast in the dining hall: three slices of bread with margarine and marmalade and hot chocolate. Later during the war when bread rationing started, it was replaced by hot oatmeal cooked in milk (which was considered inedible by many). I won't dwell on the food, as all I remember is that I was constantly hungry and in search of food. Not that we were starv-

Boys playing in Västraby

ing, but at the age of 13 and throughout the teens the need to replenish our energy was constant. Fortunately, I ate most of the dishes that were served, but gourmet food it wasn't. Whenever "old" Västrabyers meet and talk of the glorious past, food and its lack of quantity but especially of quality is a favorite subject.

School was a mixed bag of enlightenment, education, and wasted time, depending on the subject, but more specifically on the capabilities of the teachers.

The fact that my report card showed a couple of "*Mangelhaft*" or "*Ungenügend*," the equivalent of straight F (for failing), was more a reflection of the teacher's inability to communicate the subject matter, rather than innate stupidity on my part. Needless to say, my parents were surprised when this document was mailed to them, never having experienced this kind of problem with me before. But there were also rewarding times. I read a lot—the German authors of the early 20th century: Stefan Zweig, Thomas Mann, Werfel, Wassermann, Remarque, and many more. We read Shakespeare in class, and other classics, both German and foreign.

I forgot to mention that Västraby was a German-Jewish school. All the teachers were German speaking. The only person among the 60 or more students and a dozen or so teachers who was Swedish was the teacher in gardening, Herr Ljung, the nicest of the whole bunch. The school was intended to provide Jewish children from Germany an opportunity to get some schooling away from Nazi Germany while their parents in Germany tried to arrange their emigration towards having the family reunited at the earliest possible time.

Besides getting a solid dose of good books, I started listening to classical music. There was a good radio where we could sit and listen to concerts being broadcast by various stations in Sweden and abroad. It was my introduction to listening to music which very much became part of my life. I had violin lessons for a couple of years in Wiesbaden which gave me some understanding for music. But not being able to continue those studies and also not being particularly gifted to play that instrument, I regret that I did not ever play music, yet am happy that I became a devoted listener. Education covered both the regular school subjects and some practical tasks. Gardening for both the boys and girls, carpentry for us boys and dressmaking for the girls. I enjoyed the carpentry and developed some ability to work with my hands. Later in life, a lack of interest, talent and opportunity made me strictly dependent on the manual talents of my wife and son, or friends and professionals.

Gardening meant helping with the various chores needed to plant, nurse along, and harvest whatever was grown for consumption by all of us, e.g. fruit, vegetables, and potatoes. The cherry harvest was most enjoyable. The school was located in a large park with lots of trees and meadows, and several huge cherry trees in one area which carried the most luscious fruit in summer. Cherries, and later in fall pears and apples, were a welcome addition to our often rather simple diet. Also, each student could manage his own little plot, where we grew flowers or vegetables, and I spent a lot of time and devotion towards developing one of the best plots.

Life centered not only on lessons and classes, but also on social activities which were many and varied. Heavy emphasis was placed on Jewish education, on celebrating Shabbat and all Jewish holidays. The weekend started on Friday with the cleaning of all rooms and halls, which always seemed a major undertaking. Friday evenings we attended services conducted by students and teachers. After a festive dinner *Oneg Shabbat* was the highlight of the week. Concerts, readings of plays, singing and lectures on interesting topics with everybody participating provided intellectual stimulation, fun, and a sense of community. The next day, Saturday, was relaxing. Services in the morning, walks and rest in the afternoon, music or games in the evening. Festivals like *Purim*, *Pesach*, *Shavuoth*, *Sukkoth* and *Chanukah* were major social events with costume balls, theater performances, presents, dances, and plays, all organized by the students and teachers. The lengthy preparations leading up to these events were part of the fun.

During frequent vacations and other days off we made excursions—walking or bike tours—visiting the villages, towns, castles, and lakes of Skåne, the province where Västraby was located, which is the most southern part of Sweden. During the summer of 1939, we made an eight-day bike tour, covering 350 to 400 km, and stayed in youth hostels. These travels were my first introduction to the Swedish countryside, an experience that I enjoyed with undiminished delight during all my years in Sweden, and during many visits later in life.

My Bar Mitzvah was to have been taken place in Wiesbaden on December 31, 1938. The destruction of the Wiesbaden synagogue and all the other events on November 10th caused us to postpone this event, especially once we knew that I would leave for Sweden, and that I would be able to become Bar Mitzvah in Västraby. In early March, Heinz Säbel arrived from Germany, a cantor and teacher of Jewish subjects. He gave me private lessons for a few weeks, and on April 8th, *a marvelous spring day,* my Bar Mitzvah, the first one ever for Västraby, was celebrated. Hedi and Ernst Wolf helped to make this a memorable day, and so did Heinz Säbel and all the children. A

Paul on the day of his Bar Mitzvah.
With teacher, Heinz Säbel

velvet yarmulke, still in my possession, was a gift from Susi Luft, one of the "older" girls who had returned a few weeks earlier from a trip to England. She was one of the old-timers, as Västraby had already been her home for three or four years. The yarmulke was her own handiwork, but little did we suspect that all her handiwork would follow me through life. Packages with small presents, especially *"Schmonzes,"* the Västraby term for sweets, had arrived from my parents and family, and they were much enjoyed and shared with my room comrades. Later, after the war started and *Schmonzes* packages became less plentiful, all such shipments went under the jurisdiction of a *Schmonzes* minister (Secretary of Sweets), and were evenly distributed among all children. That Peter Uhl became the Candy Secretary was a foregone conclusion because he seemed to be the re-

Girls at Västraby, 1937. Susi Luft is at far left

cipient of more goodies than anyone else, and besides he exuded the right kind of authority and business talent to administer such difficult collection and distribution tasks.

Besides packages, there were many letters and cards, and I translate some of them:

My dear Paul,

Now the day that we looked forward to for such a long time, has finally arrived, and I send you my best wishes. For more than a year we made plans and talked about it, how we would celebrate this event, we even discussed the desserts and dishes to be served. But I suppose that you don't miss much in this respect, and I am only sorry that I cannot join you for the festivities. But we can be glad that you in view of present conditions are no longer here. and that you are well taken care of there.......Have a wonderful day and be glad that you can do it there....   Your Papa

My dear Paul,

My most heartfelt wishes and congratulations for your Bar Mitzvah. Stay healthy and may you become a decent person always doing what is right. We are sorry not to be able to listen to what you learned under the direction of Mr. Säbel, please tell him our thanks for his teachings and efforts. .... The Pessach days have come and gone, we had no Seder, we were alone with Oma, but drank a glass of wine thinking of all our loved ones in the world....Have a wonderful day much love for our Jewish man Paul from his Mutti

My dear Paul,

Your special day has arrived, and though I regret that I cannot personally congratulate you, so am I happy that you are there safely with Hedi and Ernst and among nice fellow students. So let me express all my good wishes for you now at the occasion of your Bar Mitzvah with the words "Jevorechecho es Adonai"........ Your Oma

Dear Paul.

Your parents a few days ago informed me that you will celebrate your Bar Mitzvah next Saturday, so I don't want to miss sending you my congratulations. It would have been nice if we could have celebrated this event together with all our family as you always wanted it. But I know that you are mature and sensible so that you know that there could not have been a better Bar Mitzvah gift for you than the fact that your parents took care to make sure that you can celebrate this day in Sweden. You must know that many thousands of your contemporaries here are envious of your good fortune. So if your thoughts on this special day occasionally turn back to your family and your former home, remember that we too think of you, and that we are glad to learn from your letters that you are so well taken care of.

We all hope so very much that the time you are spending there is to your benefit for your growth and development. You have the opportunity to achieve this, and it is up to you to make it happen.

Our unusual and abnormal era puts demands on you children which we in happier years did not experience at such a young age. But I am convinced that you will meet the expectations of all of us.

55

You won't disappoint us, and you will do honor to the name of our family of which you are the only Jewish representative among the younger generation.

At the occasion of this special day I wish you what is no doubt also your greatest wish, that we all will be reunited in the not too distant future. Even if the prospects for this to happen are so far not very favorable, we do not want to give up hope. So enjoy this day with your friends, and write us all about it very soon. I wish you the very best for your future life and send you my kindest regards.

Your Uncle Josef.

Other memories from Västraby: we were children, playing and fooling around, fighting and kidding each other, yet acting responsibly when necessary. Talking about fooling around, it included such grandiose events like carrying lit-up stink bombs to one of the girls' rooms on the upper floor of the building, or on another occasion coming back from a vacation biking trip with left-over bags and sacks with cocoa, flour, and sugar, and engaging in a pillow fight with those sacks, which of course opened up and engulfed the room in an unholy mess. These actions carried heavy penalties. The carrying of lit candles to deliver the stink bombs represented a fire hazard. So the reward was heavy labor for one week, when we had to carry heavy rocks and dig ditches. My diary identifies this week only as "*Arbeitswoche.*" To clean up our room and to try to eliminate all traces of flour, sugar and cocoa from floors, shelves, bed covers, and bed springs was a most tedious task, and although there certainly were other penalties, I only recall the endless efforts to get rid of the mess.

Bedrooms were identified by their dominant colors, e.g. the RED room, the BLUE room. Our room was the BROWN room, and we developed our own language. Not by design or intent. It just developed. An interesting case study for linguists. Eventually, it was identified as the *"Bruennsch"* (obviously for Brown) language, recognized by everyone in the school, but spoken and understood only by its practitioners: eight energetic and obviously talented juveniles. Passions reigned supreme, for a while Fredi and I would play the card

Preparing food. Fredi Hahn at left, Paul at right

game "Sixty-six" at all possible and impossible times of the day, preferably during five or ten minute breaks between classes. During the long winter of 1939-40 when it did not stop snowing, we seldom missed peeing someone's initials from our window into the snow below. That our cook had her room in the basement with her window right at snow level made the task more intriguing.

We children had our own government structure, called the *Schulgemeinde* which elected its own officials (e.g. the Candy Secretary mentioned above). I had a brilliant government career in this organization. Already on March 9, 1939, I was elected to the demanding office of *Klingel- und Tafelwart,* and although I don't remember the precise functions that this office demanded, I presume that I had to make sure that the bells were ringing for classes and other specific events both on time and loudly, and as to the table keeper it may have involved seating arrangements or making sure that the tables in the dining hall were properly arranged. Marianne Kaye, now in London, fondly remembers her career as the *Geburtstagswart,* the keeper of birthday dates who had to make sure that the birthday songs were sung for the right person on the right day. Several months thereafter, I was elected to the highest office, serving on the Executive Committee consisting of four seasoned politicians who had to debate, decide, and defend actions of such significance that I don't remember them. But it prepared me for duties later in life when as a senior partner at Kenneth Leventhal & Company I served as a member of its five-man Executive Committee for more than seven years until I started my well deserved retirement.

Another recurring feature were farewells and farewell parties. Children often, at least during the first year, departed to join their families in other countries, or to start *Aliyah* going to Palestine or to commence apprenticeships, trades, or jobs. Especially impressive was the departure of eight or ten youngsters in the spring of 1939 leaving for Palestine. After all, the school and its occupants, both teachers and children, had become one family, at times unruly and fighting, but then again devoted to each other. In other words, we were a typical family, even though a bit large.

The concentration on Jewish subjects and traditions included a strong emphasis on Zionism with migration to Palestine as the primary solution to the so-called "Jewish problem."

Paul with Georg Herzfeld, March 1940

The lectures, readings, songs and the youngsters who prepared for and actually made *Aliyah* had quite an emotional allure and convincing impact on many. I did not get caught up then or later in those ideas. My desire was to join my family in the USA as soon as we could make it. And I could not quite get enthused by anything that was nationalistic, even though I recognized the necessity and logic of creating a Jewish state. Also, in those days *Aliyah* to Palestine and the hope for a Jewish state always included a strong dose of communal living, socialism, and individual sacrifice for the greater good. And again, while I intellectually accepted the righteousness if not wisdom of all this, I knew or I sensed that this was not for me.

One important entry in my diary was on May 10, 1939. I got a haircut from Mr. Gluecksman, our carpentry teacher. Before then, I went for a haircut to the barber in the nearby village of Löberöd, which took away part of my weekly allowance of one kronor. This was real money, and allowed for occasional purchases of Danish pastries, rolls and sausages, all purchased on excursions to the nearby village of Löberöd. These were welcome refreshments to augment the less than inspiring school menus.

Summer days were often spent at the Ringsjö, a large lake a few miles away from us, where we enjoyed beach living. Also, occasional excursions to Lund visiting its sights, including a marvelous swimming hall, and EPA (a five & ten chain store) for real Swedish ice cream, were days to remember, although they were very rare except in 1940, when I had to make weekly visits there to a dentist for root canal treatments after the so-called dentist of Löberöd messed things up a bit.

In late August of 1939, the threat of war was communicated to us by daily news summaries by one or several teachers. Normally, we had such news communicating meetings only once a week. And then, on September first, while we had our usual pre-Shabbath big house cleaning event, we listened to Hitler's speech announcing the German attack on Poland. The war had begun. We hoped and prayed for Germany's downfall, especially after England and France joined Poland

Listening to radio broadcast of Hitler announcing the invasion of Poland, September 1, 1939

two days later. Two weeks later, we celebrated Rosh Hashanah, the beginning of the Jewish year 5700. A new Jewish century had begun. During the service, a violent thunderstorm almost drowned out the sounds of our prayers and the Shofar. Could it be taken as an ominous reminder of the impending destruction of European Jewry?

But life continued with its daily demands and pleasures. We had to economize, weekly allowances were cut to 10 öre, and other shortages developed. The old school automobile had to be put into storage—no gasoline. So we picked up all groceries and other necessities with our bikes.

The year of 1939 continued for us without major changes: school and play, work and festivals all came and went. In November and December I recall in my diary the tragic events of the prior year. But preparations for and the celebrations of Chanukah dominated the daily routine. On December 17 we had a big Chanukah festival. Adult members of the Jewish community of Malmö had been invited, and many other friends from the area. In other words, it was the social event of the season. Several theatrical and musical performances took place, including the playing of Hayden's *Children's Symphony*, where I played the violin, the only time that I appeared as a violin player in front of a live audience! On December 25 it snowed, and the following day I went skiing for the first time. I had brought skis from Wiesbaden, but the previous winter had been unusually mild with not enough snow to try this new sport. The winter of 1939-1940 made up for it. We had plenty of snow storms, and I quickly managed to learn to stay on my feet, or skis, and used every free hour to get out and practice. I enjoyed it immensely, and got enough of a taste to keep it up later in life for many years.

The war did not much interfere with our life. The *Blitzkrieg* in Poland and the *Sitzkrieg* on the Western front did not impact us other than reading about them or listening to the news. The Russian attack on Finland and Finland's heroic and initially successful defense caused us some concern, because events were getting closer to us. I ended the year on December 31 by skiing both morning and afternoon, and listening to a radio concert in the evening, followed by some fun festivities past midnight. My diary starts 1940 with the wish for getting to the USA and a reunion with my family during that year, and happiness for having left Germany one year earlier.

In March of 1940, Finland and the Soviet Union concluded an armistice agreement, and it appeared that peace had been restored in Northern Europe. But on April 9, we got the shocking news of the German invasion of Denmark and Norway. We didn't know what would happen next, but we had to get our bicycles and backpacks in order in case we had to run away, should the war come to southern Sweden. In retrospect, I don't know if and how we could have escaped, but I guess it was prudent to be ready if the worst was going to happen. Well, things settled down, and again routine took over. Not until May 1 did the last snow disappear. In the meantime Hedi and Ernst Wolf had left Västraby, as disagreements with Mrs. Levy, the administrative head of the school, had caused a situation where either Ernst or Mrs. Levy would remain as the director. Student upheaval and protests in support of Ernst were to no avail. The decision makers in Stockholm, leaders of Stockholm's Jewish community, had decided in favor of the person who presumably had the best managerial capabilities, rather than the higher academic background. This was upsetting to me, as I was very close with Hedi and felt sorry for them. They took jobs as gardeners in some nearby nursery. They left on May 7.

On May 10, more ominous events took place. Germany invaded Holland and Belgium, and started its attack on France. We had heard much about the great defense capabilities of both Holland and Belgium, and hoped for decisive victories by the great French army. We listened to the daily news bulletins, always hoping against hope for a last minute miracle, but the debacle in Western Europe was complete. The British evacuation at Dunkerque seemed just another major disaster, but ultimately it contributed to Britain's survival and Germany's defeat.

Another sunny and pleasant summer in Skåne with bike trips and swimming in the Ringsjö, an abundant cherry harvest, leisurely days and enjoyable activities. But Västraby is going to be closed. The older children will go to work, the younger ones (and I belong to that group) will go to a home in Northern Skåne, under the leadership of Mrs. Levy. She and the cook will be the only adults; we are going to be 20 or 25 children. It is uncertain if I will go to the Swedish elementary school or go to work. The preparations for the move take up much of everybody's time. Also, I have to go to Lund to see the dentist every week; a lengthy root canal treatment gives me the opportunity to enjoy life in the Big City! September 1, 1940 is the first anniversary of the outbreak of the war. Germany reigns supreme over most of Europe, and the future is uncertain. Emigration seems more doubtful, but at barely 15 life has much to offer me, and the impending move with all its turmoil keeps us involved and busy. Hedi and Ernst, who work not too far away from Västraby are getting visas for the U.S. and will soon leave Sweden, travelling via Moscow, Vladivostok, Japan and Hawaii. There is no transportation across the Atlantic, but they are happy to escape Europe. They spend several days prior to their departure in Västraby, arranging for Ernst's mother (who had been in Västraby for over a year) to go to an old age home in Malmö. I used to keep her company quite often, since she did not have much contact with other people. And while Hedi and Ernst were in Malmö, I find her asleep in her room in the middle of the day, and am unable to awaken her. She has taken an overdose of sleeping pills, is rushed to the nearest hospital, and dies the following day. A hectic, tragic, and tumultuous goodbye to Hedi and Ernst and to all the friends and teachers who did not join us in the new home in Osby.

An exciting and worthwhile period, almost two years, had come to a conclusion, filled with new impressions and experiences during a unique period in history and in my own life. I made friends for life; they became family. I became more independent and developed interpersonal skills. I was not terribly spoiled when I left Germany, but I certainly got used to a new level of frugality. Shortcomings in the quality of schooling and lack of parental love and guidance were compensated by the exposure to a stimulating intellectual and cultural atmosphere, to manual pursuits, to nature and scenic beauty all far removed from the sad and deteriorating life in what used to be my home. Two years I would not have wanted to miss. Only the disaster that went on beyond Sweden's peaceful shores kept us worried about an uncertain future.

OSBY

On October 15, 1940 we go by bike to Höör, a nearby town with a railway station where the trains stop that go north. After a short enjoyable train ride we arrive in Osby, some 100 km from Västraby in the northern province of Skåne. Our new home is a building in the tiny community of Ebbarp, a small group of homes and farms a couple of kilometers from Osby. Here, the landscape is more like the rest of Sweden, forests and lakes, with a few fields in between. Not the wide-open spaces of central and southern Skåne with its huge farms and endless vistas. The Osby lake is just across the road, maybe 50 or 100 meters from our home. The home has two large bedrooms, one each for the girls and the boys, and a nice sized study hall and an equally good sized dining hall. In addition, there are rooms for the two adults, Mrs. Levy and Miss Schlesinger, the cook, plus one or two tiny additional rooms for guests or sick children. One indoor toilet and bath, for the adults. We use the outdoor facilities, somewhat chilly in winter and rather smelly in summer. A shower room in the basement assures adequate cleanliness.

I do not know what I am going to do. I am almost too old to start at *folkskolan* where children go from age 7 to 14 or 15. Maybe I will have to work on a farm or in a nursery. Initially, we are kept busy with getting the house and garden in shape, a major task. Frequent truck loads had arrived from Västraby with furniture and all other belongings, and it all has to be put in place and made to function so that we have livable quarters for a couple of dozen people.

On November 1, Dr. Moritz, the school principal of Västraby after Ernst Wolf's departure, comes and announces that Georg Herzfeld, Fredi Hahn, Ruth Pordes and I will be admitted to *Osby Samskolan,* a private high school, with a four year program for ages 12 to 16. The school agreed to tuition of only 40 kronor per semester instead of the normal 120 kronor. This generous offer was accepted by the Jewish authorities in Stockholm, and the next day the four of us get introduced to the principal of the school, Rektor Ernestam. Fredi gets into

Realskolan: **school Paul attended in Osby, Sweden**

the first grade, Ruth the second, and Georg and I the third. I am delighted that I can go back to school, at least until the end of the school year in the summer of 1941. Of course I am apprehensive; our Swedish is extremely deficient. Only during the most recent months was Swedish added to the Västraby school curriculum, and those lectures were not taken too seriously, consistent with the general lackadaisical approach to our studies at that time.

November 4th: First day in school. I like it very much. We get along very well with the other students, and the teachers are very nice. We can understand everything fairly well, but talking is still very difficult. School starts in the morning at 8:30 with a 15-minute religious service with singing of psalms, reading from the Bible with commentaries and lectures. Then classes until 11:20, and again from 12:20 until 3:00. Sometimes sport or lectures in the afternoon until 5:00.

I start to study a lot. I have to play catch-up on subjects like Chemistry, Physics, Math, Geometry and History, and especially Swedish. On my 15th birthday, December14, a Saturday, there is a big Christmas or Santa Lucia party in the large school gymnasium in the evening from nine to after midnight with all sorts of plays, music, and refreshments. I enjoy every minute. On December 19, the last school day, parents are invited to attend classes. I am called upon to read an essay I wrote in Swedish dealing with the Franco-Prussian war of 1870-1871. My Swedish apparently had improved rapidly after only six weeks. At home we get ready with preparations for Chanukah, which started on December 24. *In the evening we open our presents. Lots of Schmonzes* (sweets), *letters from Helen and Susi L. and a package with a scarf from S.L.* I don't remember when Susi and I started to correspond. It may have been at the suggestion of the Wolfs when they visited the Lufts in Stockholm on their way to Finland, Russia and beyond. I use the Christmas vacation to study hard. Karl Greger, one of the older children who is taking correspondence courses towards high school graduation, helps me with French lessons.

On December 31 we light the eighth Chanukah candle. Mr. Levy on a visit brings a new record, Suppe's *Poet and Peasant Overture*. Whenever I listen to this piece of music, I remember the cold and clear New Year's night, when I prayed for peace and victory for beleaguered England. During the preceding and following months this stubborn island country had its finest hour. We listened to the German

Sawing wood, 1941. Georg Herzfeld second from left, Paul at right

broadcasts by the BBC, and gained new hope that the country might prevail in what a few months earlier had seemed a lost cause for them and us. My second year in Sweden was coming to an end. I had reached a new stage in my life. To become a serious student at the Swedish *Samskola* was a new challenge. Not since my days at the Nazi *Gymnasium* in Wiesbaden, where I wanted to excel for different reasons, had I been that much stimulated and motivated to absorb knowledge and to perform well.

Thinking back to those years in Västraby and Osby, I can say without hesitation that I was never homesick. Of course, I missed my family, but regular mail, usually one letter and a postcard each week kept me informed on how and what they were doing. I wished and hoped for a reunion in the U.S., but did not agonize over the delays and apparent difficulties to achieve this. I felt sorry for them, even though I did not fully comprehend their dreary and demeaning life, so filled with disappointments and harassment.

1941 was an uneventful year. I studied a lot and made good progress in school. My Swedish kept improving, and I managed to catch up and keep up on all other subjects. Towards the end of the spring semester, I was happy to learn that we could stay in the *Samskola* for another year. There had been doubts, especially since all children who were just a few months older than I went to work on farms, nurseries, factories, or households. The choices were limited and uninspiring. The early part of 1941 was quite cold, and we went ice-skating a lot until it started snowing in mid January, when we switched to skis. The walk to school, approximately three or four km, was shortened by skiing across the Osby lake, not always an enchanting experience when the temperature was way below zero. When spring arrived the news was dominated by the German victories over Yugoslavia and Greece, and their successful exploits in North Africa. The news became more ominous in June when the Germans started their attack against the Soviet Union. With Finland on the German side, recapturing territory lost in the winter war, war again had come closer to Sweden. But the rapid advances of the Germans and their cohorts moved the war far to the East, and again Germany appeared victorious. Summer was pleasant. I worked a lot in the garden and helped with many other domestic chores, but also enjoyed swimming in the lake, or going out in a rowboat or canoe. I made a six-day bike trip with a friend to Malmö,

Skiing. Paul and Robert Saberski

where we visited the Säbels, on to Landskrona to see Erwin Leiser, and up to Ängelholm to visit Otto and Manfred Schwarz (formerly from Wiesbaden). We slept in a tent, got soaked in the rain, and had a great time. In Malmö, we went to the movies, saw *Rebecca*, and I fell in love with Joan Fontaine. We read about the North Atlantic meeting between Churchill and Roosevelt and were encouraged by the USA's support of England's fight.

Sept. 1: Two years war—At least more hope for a favorable ending than we had last year, but less hope for an early ending as we had hoped two years ago.

Rosh Hashanah we biked to the town of Kristianstad, stayed in a hotel, attended services, and were invited for meals by the local Jew-

Paul, August 1941

ish families. The hotel was of such quality that several of us, primarily the girls, returned with lice. A major hair cutting followed. Much excitement! On Yom Kippur we stayed in Ebbarp. A few days later we all went and saw the Disney film *Pinocchio*. While in Västraby, we saw *Snow White* when it played in Löberöd.

In late October, my parents sent me the sad news that Uncle Karl suddenly died of a heart attack. He was the oldest Kleinstrass brother. Little did we know then that his death would spare him the fate of his five other brothers and sisters during the next couple of years.

Sunday evening, December 7: We are already in bed, it's 10 o'clock in the evening, we hear the news that Japan attacked the USA. The world war has now really started.

On December 13, there is a big Christmas-Santa Lucia festival at school again, from six in the evening until midnight. While we watch the theatrical performances and listen to the singing and playing, one of my teachers talks to me. He mentions that the news from the Eastern front reported that about 60,000 men were killed in just one day during the fierce battle outside of Moscow. All this, while we enjoy the Swedish holiday season!

December 14 is my 16th birthday. I get mail from all the family, except from Helen. Mail to or from the U.S. is temporarily disrupted. And I get presents from friends both at Ebbarp and elsewhere, including leather mittens from Susi Luft from Stockholm. But also woolen mittens from Alice, my local friend with whom I shared occasional walks and talks. And Chanukah is being celebrated with the exchange of small gifts, and another New Year's Eve with music and cake, celebrating the arrival of 1942, a year not to be forgotten.

Sunday Jan 4: I wish for a happy 1942! A successful ending of the war. Better living conditions for my parents. And the opportunity for me to continue higher education.

Winter starts with a vengeance. The first couple of weeks of the New Year there is hardly any snow, so we skate a lot on the lake. Then snow and freezing temperatures start. On January 25, it is minus 27 degrees Celsius. The next day, Monday, it drops to minus 35. We stay at home. It is too cold to ski across the lake to get to school. On Tuesday, it is only minus 30 degrees, and we make it to school. I remember crossing the lake on skis in temperatures between minus 20 and 30 degrees, arriving at our destination with blocks of ice in our faces caused by the instant freezing of our breath. We are lucky that nobody stumbled and got injured because to be caught outside without being able to move, could have been disastrous. The harsh winter is actually a blessing. For the first time, the German *Blitzkrieg* has been stopped, and the Nazi armies had to retreat just when they were within sight of the city of Moscow. However, it is only a temporary defeat, and more than three years of fierce fighting is still to come, with all the major tragedies yet to happen.

I am worried what will happen to me when school ends in June. The usual possibilities of going to work on a farm or in a factory or at some other low level task have little appeal. I want to continue high school for three more years, which will get me to the *studentexam*. But I lack connections to get the financial support needed for such studies. In the meantime, I am studying hard to achieve good results in the *realexam* which is coming up in a few months.

On Jan.9 I get a letter at last from Helen. It was written on Nov.24 for my birthday. U.S. entry in the war caused such delays.

During February we have several days of blackouts as an exercise for Sweden to be prepared in case of being attacked. The political events are rather sad. The Japanese successes are surprising and disappointing. The British are stalled in North Africa, and the Germans have managed to stabilize the Russian front and are preparing for a major offensive.

March 8. Today Dad has his 59th birthday, he is getting rather old. But I hope that next year we will be together again. Little do he or I suspect that it will be his last birthday. *The news from Wiesbaden continues to be ok, but I don't get any mail from Helen.*

The harsh winter continues. We celebrate Passover in early April. *It is ice cold.* Georg, Fredi, Franz, and I organize a Seder, and it turns out well. We get a sumptuous dinner, which is a special event. The war-time rationing of food and the limited funds that the home received allowed normally for only simple meals with lots of cabbage and potatoes, and very little meat. But we do not starve.

April 11: Aunt Frieda (father's sister) *deported. One feels so helpless. Everything is so awful.*

I talk with Mrs. Levy (the director of the home) *about my future. She thinks that a continuation of my studies is impossible, and she will not recommend or support it.*

April 19: Finally the snow is melting! We have much work outside and in the garden, it takes valuable time away from our studies.

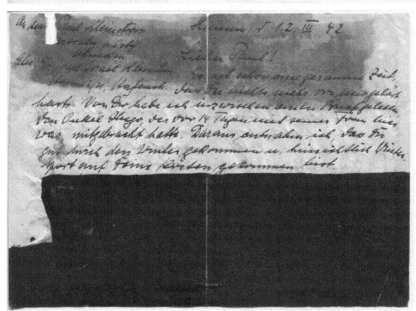

**Letters from Germany: letters from Uncle Josef Kleinstrass showing
sections blacked out by German censors**

The lake is free of ice. How beautiful it is when the sun sparkles on the water the first time since October

Franz. Arnheim, an official from the Jewish Congregation in Stockholm, visits us and talks to me about my future: *Mrs. Levy had told me that I have to talk to him, and that I should come with precise plans to pursue some apprenticeship or work. I have no intention of following her instructions. The same day I had a letter from Hedi and Ernst, and Ernst gave me the good advice to set a goal and then pursue it. And if it does not go the easy way, use detours and other means to achieve it. So I tell Mr. Arnheim that I want to continue Gymnasium studies. He sounds encouraging and will explore ways to help.*

In early May, the written examinations take place. It is the culmination of a concentrated effort to do well. The exam lasts four days, one day each for Swedish composition, math, English, and German.

May 5. Sad news from home. Aunt Minna and Uncle Josef (father's sister and brother) *are scheduled for deportation. What is still all going to happen?*

One of the boys gets scarlet fever. We are just a couple of weeks away from the oral examination. I never had scarlet fever before, and I am scared that I may catch it and be unable to finish school. We have to stay home for a week, to make sure we don't get sick too. The weather is great; we work in the garden part of the day, and study the rest.

The results of the written exam are okay, only disappointing in English where I get a B. On May 29, we are told the subjects for our oral examination. For me it is chemistry, biology, religion, and German. A last rush to study early morning and late at night, and on June 5 the oral exams take place. I do reasonably well and finally by four o'clock in the afternoon we shake hands with our teachers and the state examiners, put on our grey caps, and march out in the school's courtyard. It is crowded with well-wishers who hang lots of flower bouquets around our necks.

On a horse-drawn carriage with much hurrah and hello we go to the photographer in town for the class picture. Then Georg and I march happily but exhausted back to the Ebbarp home. Finally finished, at last after so many weeks, or rather many months, real leisure

Graduation from *Realskolan*, Summer, 1942. Paul is in the back row, second from the left; Georg is next to him

time! ...On Saturday at 7 o'clock in the evening we attend a big dinner party at the town's hotel for teachers and students. It was a wonderful event that lasted until 1:00 a.m. Then we took a nice walk along the lake and got home after 2 o'clock......On June 9th I am for the last time in the nice old school building. The final graduation exercise and the end of the school year are being celebrated. There are speeches, handing out report cards and awards. As the sixth in a class of more than thirty I receive 100 kronor, a gift from the school and the teachers. I am reasonably satisfied with my report card, even though I wish I had done better in a few subjects. And the 100 kronor are not to be sneezed at, even though I realize the charitable intent. But each one gets what is best for him. A final handshake with teachers and students, "good-bye and good luck," and I have reached the end of a wonderful one-and-one-half year period. On the way home I keep wondering what I am going to do next. Probably some work during the summer, and then hopefully more studies. I decide to join Georg, Fredi and some of the other boys and work in the peat fields, where one presumably can make good money. But it is raining until midsummer, and we could only work for two days, making 6 kronor each day. Better than nothing!....... On June 13 I get a letter from Mrs. Heyman (the lady in charge of the children's committee at the Jewish Community in Stockholm) that further studies are not available. She suggests that I take a job in an office. I am forced to agree, but only if I can get such a job in Stockholm where I would be able to continue to study at night. This correspondence kept going for some time. In the meantime, after the midsummer holiday, the weather improved and we were able to work in the peat fields every day. For eleven days of work I earned 80 kronor, for which I bought myself a second-hand bicycle. My old one from Germany I gave as a trade-in.

I remember the backbreaking work in the peat fields, the long bike ride to and from this job, and the relief in late afternoon to get home and swim in the lake, and relax in the water. And the few weekends, when we would rest up and enjoy the long Swedish summer days and the beautiful surroundings with nature at its glorious best. I was happy and hopeful, often oblivious of what went on in the world around us, preoccupied with my own concerns and expectations for my future. At age 16, one's concerns are primarily one's own, and I was no exception.

On July 10 I get a phone call from Mrs. Heyman: I can get a job as errand boy at the Jewish Community in Stockholm, which would give me enough time to study on the side. I accept, and two days later on a Sunday I leave Osby. Packing has to be done in a hurry, everything is like a dream, and yet it is happening. It is raining cats and dogs, it makes it easier to say goodbye....Fredi and another boy take me to the station. A last look at Osby, and the train takes me from a secure and orderly existence to an unknown future. May it be for the best!

STOCKHOLM

In Stockholm Peter and Georg meet me at the station. They take me first to Slöjdgatan 9 where I meet Mr. Berthold Ehrenreich (Herbert Leitner's uncle). And then we go to Hornsgatan 75, where Peter also lives. It is a regular apartment where 12 boys have their home. The first impression is less than favorable. 2 bedrooms, 1 dining room, and kitchen. That's it! In the evening I take a walk to a park overlooking Lake Mälaren and the city of Stockholm....

Monday July 13 I start my job. Everybody seems quite nice, and

Paul with Georg Herzfeld, 1942. Paul and George remained best friends throughout their lives. George lived two blocks from Paul in Los Angeles until George's death in 2012.

the work load is not overwhelming. In the evening I talk to Georg, we want to rent a furnished room. Then I meet Susi Luft, I had talked to her already on the phone the previous evening. She is quite nice and pleasant to talk to. We went for a walk, and then to the Luft's apartment. It was an enjoyable evening. I got home by 11:30. The first week went very well, it is not so difficult to find one's way in Stockholm, and I manage to do it quite quickly.

The first few weeks in Stockholm are enjoyable. I meet old and new friends, also an elderly couple from Wiesbaden, Mr. and Mrs. Siegel, who invite me often to their apartment on Gärdet. I start going to the movies, a habit that became quite prevalent during my Stockholm years. One of the first movies I go to see is *Gone with the Wind*. I also use my free time to read a lot. I get the books from the public library. I read *Buddenbrooks*, and then *The Good Earth* and *Gone with the Wind*, both in English. At first I make frequent use of the dictionary, but after a while it becomes quite easy. I get my teeth fixed which was very necessary. I am often together with Georg, Peter, and Susi. We go on our bikes to Drottningholm, rent a rowboat, and enjoy the lovely summer days. I do all my commuting on my bike, and a good deal of my job is to ride a bike, making deliveries, picking up mail, collecting documents and signatures from various offices and dignitaries. It gives me an almost instant familiarity with the city, with many of its landmarks and institutions, with quite a few of its people from all levels of society, and with its businesses and government offices. I get invited over a weekend to a Miss Warburg (a member of the Stockholm branch of the Warburg family) at her summer residence out at Lake Mälaren. She is a lovely elderly lady who has made her spacious home available for us refugee children to spend our weekends and vacations in beautiful surroundings, with lots of swimming, eating, talking, and relaxing.

Georg and I are busy room hunting, and by August 18 we have found one on Lästmakaregatan 20. *It is quite nice, the monthly rent is 70 kronor, not bad....it is great to have some privacy again.* "Quite nice" it seemed at the time. It was a spacious room, with no running water, and the toilet was in the attic of the building, and it was as primitive as the outhouse in Ebbarp. The room was adequate—anyhow, hot water did not exist during the war years, and cleanliness was achieved by going once a week to a public bath.

Susi Luft and her brother, Werner

Paul Kester

Bad news. On Saturday, Aug. 22, during dinner (I still took my dinners at the Hornsgatan boys' home) I get a postcard from Wiesbaden telling me that they all must go to Theresienstadt. So this had to happen after all. I feel helpless and depressed. I had a wonderful day that Saturday. I went to the synagogue in the morning, in the afternoon I biked by myself to Mälarhöjden for a swim and a rest in the sun, it was great being there. But these news cause me much anxiety...

October 23, 1942: It's been two months since I wrote down my last comments. Much has changed in the meantime. Since Sept. 1, I have my main meal once a day at Schrager's, a "matsal" (serves fixed meals to regular customers who buy a subscription on a monthly basis). It cost 1.50 kronor a day. The events here during the last two months are not of major consequence. My work is the same, only now there is much more to do. I spent the high holidays attending services which were very solemn and festive. My thoughts were very much with my loved ones. The first New Year's evening I was invited at Siegels. It was very "gemütlich," and I felt at home. The second evening I was invited to Cantor Bornstein's with Georg, his father, the two brothers Ehrenreich and some other gentlemen, and it was really nice. Erev Yom Kippur Mr. Herzfeld (Georg's father) invited me to a meal at a Jewish lady's who was in the business of preparing meals for this kind of special occasion. During services the next day in the synagogue Mr. Myerson asked me to join his family to break the fast. (He is a member of the Board of Trustees of the Jewish Community and a successful manufacturer). The dinner at their elegant apartment in Östermalm was nice and interesting. There was a large family gathering, including several young people. How carefree these people are!

In October I went to the Concert Hall, Endre Wolf played Beethoven's violin concerto, it was outstanding. So I made sure to go to the next concert: Mozart's Jupiter Symphony, something by Richard Strauss, and then Beethoven's Fifth. It was wonderful to let the music move me to a different world, to dream, to forget for a short while the reality of our daily lives. One needs once in a while to forget this reality, and not be consumed by one's worries and concerns.

The first six months in Stockholm were exciting. I adjusted very quickly to life in the big city. In late August I started to go to evening school, a three year *Gymnasium* leading to the *Studentexamen*. Day school would take the same three years, so it was a heavy load to manage full time work and studies. Most of the students in my class were older than I was. They had been actively working for quite a few years, and had decided to continue their education in order to secure advancement or higher positions than what they presently had. It was a nice group, and we got along splendidly.

PART 3

September 1942 to 1949 and beyond

(written in 2013)

Life in Stockholm (continued)

Two of the students separately wanted to practice their German on free evenings at dinner or during a walk on Sunday mornings, combining it with a meal that they would pay for. Money for me was in short supply, and the strict food rationing limited the purchase of inexpensive staples. The main meal described above was short on meat and bread, but potatoes were plenty, and I would often take some boiled potatoes along in my pocket and have them for dinner. But I never starved and I never felt poor. Life was interesting, and the many social contacts with friends from Västraby and Osby who also had moved to Stockholm provided family. And there were many new friends from work, the Jewish community, and at school. The one regret I had was that working full time did not provide enough time for studying.

I managed to get in contact with my parents. I wrote postcards addressed to them in Theresienstadt and sent them registered with return receipt. Within a few days I received these receipts signed by them. In spite of strict German censorship and raging war beyond our borders, mail with the neutral Sweden was kept going by the Nazis.

And when my parents after five months in Theresienstadt, and later other relatives, were transported to Auschwitz to be murdered, my letters were returned to me with *"Abgereist"* (left town) properly stamped on the envelope.

My grandmother had been sent to Theresienstadt with my parents in September 1942. She died there in May 1944. During her stay of almost two years before her death, I was able to send small packages every month and to write to her frequently. It gave her solace and hope. I am grateful that she died in Theresienstadt. She was scheduled for transport to Auschwitz, but escaped this final tragedy.

I even wrote to my childhood friend Leo Kahn. He made it to Holland when I came to Sweden, but was deported in the spring of

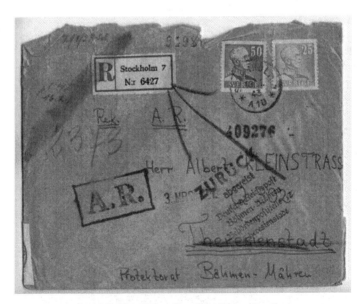

Last letter from Paul to his parents.
Stamped *"Zurück* [Return to sender]. *Abgereist* [Departed]"

<table>
</table>

Stockholm, 18 Dec. 1942

Dear Leo,

    I send you my heartfelt greetings and hope that you are healthy and in good cheer. From Lotte [Leo's sister] I hear often and she is at her old work. She is healthy and glad to have it. Your parents are together with mine [in the Theresienstadt Ghetto], I hear little but know that they are healthy.

    For me things are going well and I have lots of work. Stay brave and confident, you are young and will get through anything. Soon there will be for us all a reunion under happier circumstances.

    For you good wishes, also in the name of your beloved sister and parents I remain your friend Paul.

Postcard to Leo Kahn sent to *"Workcamp Birkenau,"* the death camp at Auschwitz. Stamped *"Concentration camp refuses acceptance Return to sender."*

1942. His older sister Lotte, doing slave labor in Berlin, sent me his new address: "Labor Camp Birkenau near Auschwitz." My card to him came back stamped "Concentration Camp refuses acceptance."

The German obsession with order and compliance with international mail regulations was remarkable!

Lotte worked in Berlin until February 1943. She was then deported directly to Auschwitz (*Fabriksaktion*) for more slave labor. She eventually committed suicide.

I kept all correspondence, or copies of several documents that I had donated to the Jewish Museum in Berlin. Letters from my family during the years 1939 to September 1942 are still in my possession. They were copied and are in archives in Wiesbaden, the town where we lived in Germany, and from where I had been fortunate to escape. They are being read at memorial events, more recently in my presence at a memorial exhibit in Wiesbaden's town hall. English translations are in my files, to be kept by my family. My son, daughter-in-law, and two grandchildren know all about our history, and are touched by the tragic events of the Holocaust and the fates of our family.

There were two events during my first year (1942-43) in Stockholm that could have greatly changed my life if they would have been successful. One was my going to the British Embassy in Stockholm and trying to volunteer for military service. I felt I should join the fight against the Nazis. In view of what was happening to my family and friends caught in the Nazi murder machine, I could not idly sit by in Stockholm while others were fighting my battle. The Embassy accepted my application, but informed me that citizens of its Allied countries, e.g. Norway, Poland, Holland, and France, would have first claim on transportation to England. With Sweden being surrounded by Germany and German-occupied countries such transportation consisted only of small planes flying secretly across Nazi territory. When I was finally notified that it was my turn sometime in 1944, the war was in its last stage, and I was too much settled in Sweden and tied down with studies to change my life so completely.

The second event happened in early January 1943. The lady at the Stockholm Jewish Community in charge of us refugee children called me one day to her office. There I was introduced to a Mrs. Carleson from the town of Degerfors, located in western Sweden close to its border with Norway. She offered to have me join her family. Her son was my age, also a *Gymnasium* student, and I would be able to become again a "daytime" student. I liked Mrs. Carleson and accepted her generous offer. However, she mentioned that there were two issues that could jeopardize my move to Degerfors to join the Carleson family. One was a physical checkup to make sure I was healthy. The other was permission by the Swedish authorities for my move to Degerfors. I passed the physical checkup, but the application for me moving was rejected. Degerfors was located in an area that apparently was restricted for foreigners, and I, a 17-year-old school kid, maybe could have presented a serious security risk for Sweden. If the Swedish bureaucracy had been more flexible and allowed my joining this well-established non-Jewish Swedish family, it might have changed my life considerably.

A few days after the authorities' rejection of my move I received a letter from Mrs. Carleson. She wrote (translated from Swedish):

"Degerfors, Jan.12, 1943

Dear Paul,

I would have been very happy to provide a home for you during your stay in Sweden, but unfortunately it could not be arranged. Since I liked you the moment I met you, I want instead to give you a helpful hand with the enclosed funds. I hope that they may be of help and a blessing for you. Best wishes,

Aina Carleson"

The letter contained the sum of 1,000 Swedish *kronor*, enough to pay all my living expenses for at least seven months, and it enabled me to complete my *Gymnasium* studies as will be mentioned later in these my memoirs.

So life in Stockholm continued without major upheavals or changes. Daily problems included basics like getting a winter coat, and also more warm clothing to cope with all the bike riding, which was part of my job, during the long Swedish winter months. My salary did not allow purchases of such items. But working at the Jewish Community gave me access to a Jewish clothing factory and the Used Clothes Charity Store. As I said before, I never starved. And neither did I ever suffer from the cold weather, although my wardrobe lacked variety and elegance.

Work during daytime and school at night kept me busy, but there was always time for frequent movies, occasional concerts, plays, and operas, and get-togethers with old and new friends. Stockholm during the 1940's had a thriving cultural life. Some of the most outstanding conductors, soloists, and artists had found refuge in Sweden, or came for guest appearances from war-torn countries to enjoy a brief interlude of adequate meals, hotels, stores, and bomb-free nights. Not until after the war would we attend if guest performers were from Germany. I followed the events of the war in great detail. One thousand bombers over Cologne, 1200 over Essen, thousands over other German cities caused happy notations in my diary. The victories in North Africa, the bloody German defeat at Stalingrad, the collapse of Mussolini's regime—they all provided hope for a better day. But there were also days of dismay and despair. We learned early on what went on in the German-occupied countries. What the world didn't learn until after the war ended was common knowledge for us in Sweden when it happened. Deportation meant extermination. To be uprooted meant certain death. I still remember when the old Chief Rabbi of Sweden, Marcus Ehrenpreis, in 1942 at Rosh Hashanah started his sermon: *"A rabbi at the beginning of a new year is supposed to give his parishioners hope for the future. Today there is no hope."* And so it became clear to me that family and so many friends caught in the throes of the Nazi killing machine were gone forever, and remained for me only as a treasured memory from my childhood days.

But youth looks ahead, and it is in old age that we think back of what happened and what could have been.

Paul Kester

1943 brought few changes. I had a nice three-week summer vacation, visiting the home in Ebbarp-Osby with side trips to reunite with my friends from the earlier Swedish years. In December I had my 18th birthday. I was very much grown up and managing life pretty well. Birthday presents from friends and colleagues included two ties, airmail stationery, toothpaste, cufflinks, marmalade, cheese, and sardines. Georg and I had recently moved to a *pensionat*, where we continued to share a room, and where I had my main meal of the day. We now had the luxury of a bathroom on the same floor, admittedly with only cold water, and shared it with the other six tenants. But the weekly public baths took care of personal hygiene. And I indulged in the use of a sunlamp to get a good tan, which contributed later in life to the need for dermatologists. My night studies progressed nicely, in spite of a heavy schedule. At 18, I qualified for tobacco coupons. Tobacco was severely rationed, and so were most food items. One of the staff at work bought half of my monthly allotment. It provided me with enough money to use the other half to buy cigarettes for myself. I started to enjoy smoking, and kept it up at a moderate pace until 1964, when it became known that it was not conducive to good health. Looking back at those years I am amazed at a young person's capacity to lead the kind of active life I did in those days. Working five days, school from 6:00 PM for at least three and mostly four hours, finding time for home work and extra jobs on weekends, being part of a youth group of refugee youngsters meeting on Sunday nights for lectures and socializing, and so much more. One of my more interesting extra jobs was to walk on Saturday mornings Stockholm's

94

old and almost blind Chief Rabbi Ehrenpreis from his apartment to the synagogue. He was in his eighties and would tell me about his long and fascinating life. He was one of the early Zionists, had known Theodor Herzl and many other dignitaries, attended Zionist congresses from their very beginnings and had served as rabbi in many European capitals. These forty minute walks, besides making some extra money, provided more inspiration and education than I could have gotten in any other venue.

It was in 1943 that the Nazis started deportation of Jews from Norway and Denmark. Only half of Norway's 2000 Jews managed to escape to Sweden, but when the time had come for the 7000 or 8000 Danish Jews, they could be saved across the Baltic thanks to the help of Danes and a more receptive Swedish attitude. By now it was obvious that the Allies would win the war, which eased Sweden's attitude and changed its "strict" neutrality (which included helping the German war effort with trade and transporting German troops on Swedish railroads) towards a more relaxed position in our favor.

1944 was exciting. World events gave hope for a new future. The rapid success at the Eastern front, the successful landings in Normandy, the liberation of France, the German generals' failed attempt to overthrow the Hitler murderers, it all came down to the question of how soon would it end.

I realized that it would be difficult for me to finish the *Gymnasium* within the three-year period. So I used my "connections" at the Jewish Community to get a scholarship of 1200 kronor which in addition to the 1000 kronor gift from Mrs. Carleson provided me with enough funds to quit work and study full time during the last school year. On June 30, 1944, the management and staff of the Jewish Community at a festive ceremony at its conference center presented me, their youngest employee, with a leather bound volume of "Sweden's History" with this inscription:

"To Paul Kleinstrass,

The Jewish Community is thanking you for an especially good work performance serving the Community and is wishing you much success in your future."

The first two years of my working life had come to an end. After almost four years in the countryside of southern Sweden in refugee children's homes, I had easily adjusted again to big city surroundings. Already as a child in Germany I was always quite independent and enjoyed the company not only of children my age, but always felt comfortable with adults, be they the many relatives and family friends or teachers. And so the transition to life among adults, being responsible for all the many minor and major tasks, managing my meager financial resources, taking care of daily chores like shopping and laundry, were no challenge. I was invited quite often by an elderly couple, originally from Wiesbaden, and by other families. But most of my social life was with my friends from the earlier Swedish years, among them my roommate Georg and Susi Luft. She and I had developed a liking for each other already in Västraby. We reconnected

upon my coming to Stockholm (she had moved there two years earlier) and again enjoyed each other's company. A casual friendship
eventually turned into a friendship for life, and a happy marriage.

In early 1944 I was asked at the Jewish Community to take care
of a 13-year-old boy, Dieter, (also one of the 500 children in the
Kindertransport) who lived in northern Sweden with a gentile family
and had no access to any Jewish education. So he attended religious
studies at the Community's school in the afternoon, and "worked" for
me during the earlier part of the day. He adopted me as his mentor
and older brother. He wanted me to visit him when he returned to the
far north. His confirmation took place in early June, and his "uncle"

Friends: Peter Uhl, Susi Luft, Georg Herzfeld

had come to Stockholm for the celebration. I was invited for dinner at the Grand Hotel, where the "uncle" extended an invitation for me to visit them. He was a highly educated and charming bachelor in his early 50s, who in 1939 had opened his home for two of the "*Kinder*." I gladly accepted his invitation and decided to include such a visit in my summer vacation.

I first travelled to southern Sweden, visited the friends at Ebbarp-Osby, continued to Malmö with Georg, and then joined Susi for a few days in Arild, an idyllic seaside resort on the southwestern coast of Sweden. Then I continued north for a couple of days in Göteborg,

Susi Luft

Sweden's second biggest city and major port, and on to Junsele in Ångermanland, a province in Northern Sweden. I enjoyed the gracious hospitality of Olle Högberg, Dieter's "uncle," in his large and comfortable home. It was located outside of the small community of Junsele in a forest, and Olle still had a farm with cattle and goats, besides owning large forest properties. The Ångerman River was within close walking distance, where we would swim. Two weeks in this Swedish home with its great library, delicious meals, and interesting company was an unforgettable experience. It included several days of walking through the forests, herding cattle from one grazing area to the next, sleeping in old wooden shacks, and living in untouched nature.

Paul, 1947

Back in Stockholm, I started a more concentrated study routine, now being able to spend my days catching up and getting ready for the *studentexamen* in the spring of 1945. The first written test (four hours) started March 15. I had to write an essay about "General education versus specialization—comment and explain its pros and cons." I don't remember what I wrote, but I always had good writing skills and wound up with an acceptable grade. More written exams in other subjects followed over the next two weeks. School continued until the oral exam on May 29, which was the final day of school. In the afternoon we were told that we had passed all examinations, and were met outside the school building by family, or in my case by many friends, with flowers and an exciting march to the *pensionat* where I lived, where the event was celebrated with coffee and cake, with speeches and jokes, and for me a sense of relief and accomplishment.

There was more excitement during this memorable spring of 1945. Every day brought more news of the now rapid advance into Germany by the Allies, and my diary records the fall of each major German city and eventually the death of Hitler and complete German capitulation on May 7. I quote my diary (translated from Swedish):

"May 7th, 1945, 2:15 PM-

Just now I listened to the special radio news that Germany has capitulated. A war that lasted 6 years has ended. For us Jews the war lasted more than 12 years, where we lost so much. But now it has ended—the thought that dominates. The war is finished, that is most important. The killing has ended, the terror has ended, persecutions have stopped, and we live in peace. Finally!

Now life continues. Sacrifices have been awful. I have lost much, the most a person can lose, except one's own life and existence. I don't know who of my family will have survived. Probably not many, that is certain.

Now that it all is finished I think: Never forget, never!"

The summer of 1945 was filled with parties and celebrations for us newly completed students. And there were the usual activities in our Jewish youth group, and much socializing with my many friends, but especially with Susi who had become so much a part of my life.

During the last few weeks of the war and shortly thereafter thousands of concentration camp survivors, mainly girls and young women, had been brought to Sweden. They were kept in camps and hospitals to recover from their unspeakable years of slave labor, starvation, and torture. We started visiting them to bring them hope and solace, and help them to slowly learn to start life again under "normal" conditions. Among the survivors was a friend of my mother, Lilly Baruch, from Wiesbaden who miraculously had survived Theresienstadt, Auschwitz, and Bergen Belsen. She was the only one of the hundreds of friends and family who had been part of my childhood years to survive the Nazi inferno.

I went back to work at the Jewish Community now using my knowledge of languages to write letters for those survivors who tried to contact relatives in different parts of the world. I had learned to type and could handle most Swedish and foreign correspondence.

In August I again travelled to Junsele, enjoying the wonderful hospitality of Dieter's "uncle." I loved the natural beauty of northern Sweden, and I still now dream sometimes of walking down to the river or hiking through the forests. It was in these idyllic surroundings that the news of the atom bomb reached us, but also the end of WWII.

Back in Stockholm, I started working at the Stockholm branch of the Jewish Agency, again as foreign correspondent, and in February 1946, I switched to the Jewish Community's office for assistance to help survivors with their efforts to migrate to overseas countries. Tempted to pursue journalism, I worked evenings as an intern at one of Stockholm's daily newspapers, and after a few months I enrolled in an evening class for journalism. I also conducted a class for survivors, teaching Swedish. In retrospect I marvel at the multitude of projects and tasks I managed to deal with, in addition to all other social activities. But youth's capacity for a most active life is enormous.

Travel to the United States

The urge for new experiences and the desire to see my sister and other relatives and friends in America made me begin planning a visit to the U.S. I had no money, but that would not stop me from trying. Through my contacts at the Jewish Community I knew that the Swedish Iron Ore producer, the Grängesberg Corporation, provided transportation of two or three passengers to the U.S. on each of its iron ore boats. I had met the Jewish wife of Grängesberg's president,

Mrs. Waldenström, who arranged for me to meet her husband at his office. The interview went well. The result was free passage on the m/s Saivo from Narvik, a port city in northern Norway, high above the Arctic Circle. Now I needed a visitor's visa. The U.S. consul rejected my application. He believed that I wanted to use a visitor's visa to enter the U.S. permanently. How could I convince him that I had no intention to stay in the U.S? *"Show me your return ticket,"* was his condition. So I borrowed 600 *kronor* from the Jewish Community office, bought the ticket, and got my visa. On the afternoon of June 15, 1946, I started the long train ride, more than 24 hours, to Narvik together with Inge, one of the Jewish *"Kinder,"* and a Swedish student. The three of us would be the sole passengers. The trip to Narvik through the both beautiful and endless Swedish landscape of forests and lakes, and later through the more desolate areas of Lapland eventually turned into a breathtaking ride along the mountain edge of the Norwegian fjord leading to Narvik. We boarded the ship on the evening of the 16th, settled down and had dinner with the captain and the two chief officers. Trying to go to bed at midnight with bright sunshine around us seemed strange. Two days in port, while the ship completed being loaded, included walks through Narvik, a town heavily damaged during the battles of WWII. A visit to the cemetery with its sections for members of the Allied forces and soldiers of the German army provided a stark reminder of the tragic history of recent years.

The voyage took two weeks. We passed by the Lofoten islands, impressive scenery, and then crossed the somewhat stormy North Atlantic towards sunnier southern latitudes. Our spacious cabin was first class, and the meals were great. The library onboard helped to keep us occupied, and nightly card games with the captain were fun. Both he and the officers were good company, and the two weeks turned out to be a great vacation, the experience of a lifetime.

On July 2 we reached Chesapeake Bay and landed at Baltimore. The two officers took us three passengers on a nightclub tour of Baltimore, starting at the most elegant club, and winding up in rundown bars in Baltimore's slum area. What a start in the great USA! Next morning we bade good-bye to our hosts and the crew. I took a train for a short trip to Washington, D.C. and spent the afternoon and evening on an extended walking tour of the nation's capital. Then an early (4:00 AM) train to New York. Arriving at Penn Station, I went by subway to Grand Central Station, and then took a taxi to the ferry train station and a ferry ride across the Hudson and to the town of Teaneck. There, after eight years, I was reunited with two aunts, Martha and Bertel, and later in the day with my late mother's first cousin Walter. They were amazed, amused and impressed that I had managed to come from New York to Teaneck by train; the normal commute was by bus.

I spent five weeks in Teaneck, and went most days to New York, a short bus ride to Manhattan, visiting relatives and friends formerly from Wiesbaden or Stockholm and doing much sightseeing. Its museums, theaters, skyscrapers, huge apartment buildings, giant department stores, crowds everywhere, multitudes of races and colors—I saw it all and loved its endless varieties. Friends and relatives of my parents' generation welcomed me, and it was interesting to meet them in these foreign surroundings. Some lived in simple conditions in unattractive apartments in upper Manhattan or the Bronx, others were already quite well to do in elegant apartments or villas close to fancy beach clubs and in secluded suburbs. They all were proud Americans, appreciative of the opportunities that a victorious and now prosperous country provided.

I met quite a few young people my age. They seemed less burdened by the events of the recent past, more materialistic and goal-oriented in their pursuit of careers and studies as compared to us European "children."

While in New York, I had purchased for $100 a cross country round trip bus ticket on the Greyhound lines. And so in early August 1946, I started what over the next ten weeks turned out to be a fascinating tour across the U.S. The first stop was Cleveland where I was welcomed by the Herveys, relatives of Aunt Martha, and stayed in their comfortable villa in one of Cleveland's suburbs. I got exposed to Midwestern life, centered around family, friends and work. My cousin, chief engineer at a foundry, took me to the company picnic where I admired the informality and camaraderie among the employees. The lack of class-consciousness was remarkable. One of the foremen invited me to spend the weekend with his family. His son, about my age, and I had fun flying his model airplane, going to a bowling alley, and watching part of a neighborhood baseball game. The two days with this unsophisticated friendly family in their simple house were very special and gave me an insight into the more positive aspects of life in America.

After more than a week in Cleveland, I continued my bus travel past towns with some of the country's giant heavy industries, and on into Chicago. My late mother's best friend met me, and I spent two weeks with her and her brother. I explored the city, went to its many museums, its stockyards, and street markets. I even attended a burlesque show and found it boring. I visited Chicago's Swedish newspaper office, and was invited to attend a luncheon of the Swedish American Journalist Club and spoke about Sweden in the post-war era.

The last day of August at midnight I started the long bus trip to the West Coast. Next morning we crossed the mighty Mississippi and continued through Iowa and Nebraska to Wyoming, past endless stretches of farmland, the breadbasket of the USA and much of the rest of the world, especially in those days right after WWII. A two-day stopover in Denver included a sightseeing tour of the nearby Rocky Mountains, a fascinating introduction to vast and most interesting rock formations, a landscape so different from what I had seen until then. Travelling through Colorado, New Mexico, and Arizona with side trips to the Grand Canyon and Boulder Dam was for me a once in a lifetime experience. Many pages in my diary describe the awesome vistas of mountains and canyons, of tiny towns in the desert, all endlessly fascinating. And everywhere, on the bus, in the small western communities, at hamburger joints and ice cream soda bars people of all ages and stations in life made conversation. Their easy informality and friendly curiosity established instant contact. It was one of the more attractive features of life in America.

After one week's tour through the Wild West I finally arrived in Los Angeles, and reunited with my sister Helen after more than eight years. We had parted as children and met again now as young adults, having spent the intervening years in much different surroundings and circumstances, but sharing the loss of our common home and family.

Helen had married the previous year, and she and her husband Max Henlein had recently moved to Los Angeles. Apartments were hard to get, and their new house was under construction, financed by the G.I. bill, a great help for former soldiers. They only had a rented room, and after a couple of nights on the couch in their landlady's living room I moved to the Wolfs, my distant cousins who had been teachers at Västraby and had been instrumental in getting me included in the *Kindertransport* program to Sweden. So I explored Los Angeles, spending evenings with Helen and Max, and riding the buses and streetcars covering the various sections of L.A. I also learned to hitchhike, which worked well in this town with its poor public transportation and great distances. I met and talked to many people, friends of the Henleins and Wolfs, most of them from Europe, but also people I met in this city of many races and cultures. I was impressed by the informality of the California lifestyle, its superb climate, its landscape—both its endless beaches and its hills and mountains, its sometimes crazy architecture. Here everybody was a newcomer, many if not most people had migrated from other parts of the U.S. or foreign countries, and if English was not spoken with foreign accents, then with the sounds of English easily identifiable with Brooklyn, Boston, Oklahoma, or Mississippi. Ernst Wolf was a teacher at Santa Monica High School and introduced me to the Principal, who right away had me speak to one of the high school classes. I enjoyed the freshness and easygoing atmosphere between teachers and students, and the students' uninhibited questions.

California was not only far away in distance from Europe and even New York, but also far away in people's attitudes and expectations. I had encountered some of this spirit during my days in Cleveland, and among my travelling companions I met on my transcontinental journey, but nowhere as much as under the blue skies of Southern California.

Two days in San Francisco concluded my month in California. A friend recently emigrated from Stockholm, Dieter Mamlock, gave me the grand tour of this city, one of the most beautiful and interesting cities in the U.S. From there I travelled three days and three nights on the Greyhound bus back to Chicago. I had gotten used to this mode of transportation and could sleep at night, only interrupted by rest stops every two or three hours for bathroom visits and refreshments at the cafeterias. Hamburgers, ice cream, and cold drinks became my standard meals.

When I was back for two days in Chicago, Alice Keiles took me to a stellar performance by the New York Metropolitan Opera of Rigoletto. Then another night bus ride to Cleveland and an overnight stay at the Herveys. And my last overnight trip back to New York and Teaneck and another two weeks in New York.

Two more years in Sweden, 1946 – 1948

On the first of November I boarded m/s Gripsholm for the partly stormy voyage back to Sweden. Exactly four months had passed since my arrival in Baltimore, four months of reunions, new experiences, and exciting exposure to life in the U.S. and its people. The arrival on a cold and wet and dark day in Göteborg was somewhat of a letdown. Relatives and friends in America had suggested that I stay in the U.S and not go back. The thought had never occurred to me. My home was in Sweden. But as the ship tied up at the harbor on this dismal day in Göteborg, where even the taxis were black (not like New York

Susi and Paul at wedding of Susi's sister, Eva, to Gunnar Gluckman

and the rest of the U.S. where they were yellow or green or blue), I was wondering if I had not made a mistake. But then I knew I had the option to go back, and decided that I would not deal with this issue for the next one or two years.

Back in Stockholm I resumed the many social and cultural activities with my friends. I continued my friendship with Susi, and while I was not ready to commit to plans for the future, we enjoyed being together. We belonged to various youth groups, and were active in helping the Jewish survivors become part of our life. I continued giving Swedish lessons, and also gave English lessons. I started part-time work for my friend Georg's recently widowed mother in her import

Paul and Georg, 1948

trading firm, and also in his uncle's trading company, mainly handling their business correspondence, both Swedish and foreign.

I rented a room in a nearby apartment, and enjoyed the privacy of not sharing living space with others—the first time since arriving in Sweden. I enrolled in Stockholm University wanting to study Political Science. I attended lectures and tried to pursue a demanding study program. I also worked extra hours handling foreign correspondence for several business people on a free-lance basis. It provided extra income, but left little time to comply with academic requirements. So after one or two semesters I gave it up, recognizing life's practicalities and priorities, and also realizing that the subject was not meant for me.

While the great event in 1946 for me was the trip to the USA, 1947 was highlighted by a four-week vacation to four European countries: Denmark, Holland, Belgium, and Germany. My friend Georg and I had decided to spend a couple of weeks in Holland, a country still trying to recover from the devastation of five years of Nazi occupation and exploitation. Georg had relatives in Amsterdam, and it was here that I met his cousins the Shindlers. They later immigrated to Vancouver, Canada, and they became lifelong friends of ours after we all had settled on the Pacific coast. Interesting sightseeing in Copenhagen, Amsterdam, and Brussels was interspersed with lovely sunny days in Scheveningen, a beautiful beach resort on the Dutch coast.

The train ride on the international train from Copenhagen to Amsterdam (travel by plane was rare and expensive in those days) brought me back to Germany, highlighted by riding at slow speed through the endless ruins of Hamburg, Bremen and other German cities, and by the once so proud German citizens lining up along the in-international train hoping and begging for bread or a cigarette from us well-fed and presumably rich foreigners.

An uncle of mine, Hugo, a brother of my late father, had survived the Holocaust. His wife, my aunt, was Catholic, and he was not deported to Theresienstadt until early 1945, when the Allies were already fighting on German soil, some 100 miles away from Bredenborn in Westphalia, where they lived. He survived the ordeal and made it back home. I had notified him of my trip to Holland through northwestern Germany, and he and his family met me when my train briefly stopped at Osnabrück, a town not too far from Bredenborn. I

Paul, 1947

handed them a suitcase containing food and other items not obtainable in post-war Germany, and told them that I had a visitor visa issued by the Allied Military Commission's office in Stockholm.

Two weeks later on my return trip from Brussels in the early morning I got off the international train in Osnabrück, and started my exhausting and lengthy train trip to Brakel and then by bus and hitch-hiking to Bredenborn. The following article I wrote in 1995 describes part of this first visit back to Germany:

"During the summer of 1947 I return to Germany for the first time after more than eight years. The international express train provides a comfortable trip past Hamburg, Bremen, the Ruhr district—vast territories of ruins, rubble, and debris. I visit relatives who live in a small village not far from Paderborn in Westphalia. One uncle is still alive—the only Jewish survivor of a once large family. His wife is Catholic, so he was not shipped off to Theresienstadt concentration camp until February 1945. His wife and both sons, born in 1934 and 1937, were allowed to stay at home. A 14-year-old daughter was doing forced labor in a camp. She and my uncle survived. The village looks the same as it did eight years ago—it seems like nothing has changed. No, the many Jewish relatives are gone, chased away, and murdered. The vacation paradise of my childhood years looks like it always did, only the people I loved are no longer there. And I don't care for those who live there now. They are disappointed that my uncle came back and that he now demands the return of what always belonged to him. And here I am back from Sweden. *"Oh yes, in Swe-*

den you are well off," the peasants tell me. The same ones who now get rich relieving the begging city dwellers of their few possessions in exchange for bread and produce.*

I stay in Wiesbaden for three days. Compared to other German cities, the town shows very little bomb damage. I know my way around exactly as I did eight years ago. The streets and the buildings are the same and yet I find myself in an alien town. The family and friends whom I left behind in January 1939, hoping for an early reunion, are gone long ago. A policeman in civilian clothes goes with me to visit our former apartment. The chairs, tables, beds, cabinets, carpets—they are all still there—left behind by my parents and grandmother, when they had to leave on August 29, 1942 for their last painful journey. Strangers now live in our apartment. I sense their apprehension that I have come to take things away from them. But I do not want anything. The dead do not come back (only in my dreams)—so what should I do with dead objects?"

The primitive and unbelievably overcrowded train rides in Germany, the complete lack of life's necessities, the sullen people, the rude officials—I feel a certain sense of satisfaction, that the former arrogant and cruel masters of Europe now experience some of what they had done to others. Here I was, 21 years old, demanding and obtaining service denied to others thanks to my cigarettes and dollars plus my foreign credentials.

---

* As this book was going to press, we learned that the village of Bredenborn, on the 75th anniversary of Kristallnacht, would be placing a memorial for the deported and murdered Jews of the town at the former site of the Kleinstrass house.

But I was glad to get back on the international train in Hamburg with a friendly Danish train conductor wishing me a safe trip home.

It was not until the 1980's, long after Germany had been rebuilt and again became a functioning western democracy, that new generations of Germans started to deal with their country's past. Our frequent trips to Europe during the last thirty years included many visits to Germany, where I often spoke to students about my life and childhood under Nazism, trying to explain the unexplainable, and never forgetting or forgiving the crimes committed and tolerated during their grandparents' or great-grandparents' generation.

Paul, 1948

It was a comfortable life in Stockholm. But as 1947 came to an end and 1948 started with no real challenges or opportunities for a career, I decided to emigrate to the U.S. I did not like the political situation in Europe. Western Europe was still suffering and only slowly recovering from the ravages of WWII. The Soviet Union pursued an aggressive and expansionary policy in eastern and central Europe; there was always the risk of another war. I did not like the conformity, narrow regulations, formality and restrictions existing in Sweden at that time. And being young and willing to start a new life I wrote to my family in the U.S. telling them of my plans and asking for the necessary affidavits. And so, after another memorable beautiful Swedish summer, I bid good-bye to the many friends in Stockholm and in the rest of the country, and on September 12, 1948, I started the long trip into an uncertain future. It was the end of almost ten years in Sweden, years of growing up, years of awesome and awful changes in Europe and in the lives of its people, years of destruction and mass murder. I had enjoyed the good fortune to spend this period in peaceful surroundings, but the events of those years changed and shaped my life forever.

Good-bye Europe—Hello USA

It took me almost two months to get to the U.S. I again visited my uncle and his family in Bredenborn and Paderborn. My uncle even gave me driving lessons, which was no great challenge on the then empty German country roads, but not quite enough for facing Los Angeles traffic later on! I then spent a few days in Wiesbaden dealing with authorities and my attorney, exploring how to pursue restitution and compensation for what had been stolen. But it was an exercise in futility—only fifteen years later did we receive some token payments.

I continued to Switzerland primarily to obtain a French transit visa. I had booked my trip to New York from Southampton but wanted first to visit relatives in Strasbourg. To get a visitor's visa for France was impossible, the red tape during those chaotic postwar years is hard to imagine for today's American traveler. I combined it with a five-day sightseeing tour to Zürich, Luzern, and Interlaken with a breathtaking mountain trip up the Jungfrau, Montreux and Geneva, and marveled at the country's grand and always changing scenery. And then, a short train-ride from Basel to Strasbourg where I went to visit one of my late mother's cousins, Änna Kahn. She and her husband and young daughter had managed to escape the Nazis, first to the unoccupied part of southern France, and later when the Germans also took over that part of the country, across the mountains into Switzerland. By now they were reestablished in Strasbourg, a beautiful old city relatively undamaged from the war. I spent two pleasant weeks, being with family again, and liked the company of their lovely 18-year-old daughter Lilo and her young friends.

Strasbourg was followed by ten days in Paris. Each day was crowded with lots of sightseeing and also meeting old friends formerly from Stockholm, or friends and relatives of my Stockholm "family."

Finally, on November 11, I continued my European farewell tour. I went to Dieppe, followed by a calm channel crossing to Newhaven and on to London, where I was met by another of my mother's many cousins, Liesel Kounine, and stayed a few days with this charming lady and her Russian Jewish husband. Again, I enjoyed gracious hospitality and extensive sightseeing. In contrast to Paris, London in 1948 had not recovered from the privation and damage caused by the war. But attending good theater, witnessing a session of Parliament, and passing Buckingham Palace just when the palace announced the birth of Prince Charles, the seemingly forever-future king of England, compensated for the drab November climate and people.

I had booked passage from Southampton to New York on the Queen Elizabeth, then the world's biggest and fastest ship, anticipating a quick five-day crossing. But it took 17 days, the first twelve days in the port of Southampton. A longshoremen strike in New York caused the delay, providing an extra vacation on board ship with good food, movies, and nice company with lots of young people.

We arrived in New York at night, where the skyline of the city all lit up provided a glorious welcome to the New World. I stayed with my mother's cousin, Walter Baum, for a couple of weeks, visited friends and relatives, and then continued to Cleveland. Here, I obtained my social security card and registered for the draft, military service being obligatory in the States until the early 1970's. My relative Eugene Hervey and I discussed my future, and upon his advice I changed my name from Kleinstrass to Kester. To change last names in Sweden would have been a lengthy and expensive legal procedure. In Cleveland we did it in half an hour by looking for an easy name in greater Cleveland's phone book. When I applied for my Social Security card, I started to explain to the lady official that my legal name was Kleinstrass, but that I wanted to use the name Kester. Whereupon the lady told me *"Don't tell me your life's story—what name am I supposed to type?"* I was amazed at the lack of red tape and the ease of getting things done. Only in America!

Eugene suggested that I should continue to Los Angeles and get married. Susi had arrived in Los Angeles some weeks earlier, and now accepted my proposal by phone. I had not wanted to marry with no job, no money, and no profession, but my cousin convinced me

Wedding of Susanne and Paul Kester, January 6, 1949

that I was now in the USA where these details did not matter! Besides, married men were not being drafted, which provided an extra incentive to give up my bachelor status. And so I took the three-day train trip in early January 1949 from the freezing Midwest to sunny California, where the day upon my arrival Susi and Paul became husband and wife in a simple ceremony at Los Angeles City Hall. Today, in 2013, we can look back on more than 64 years of married life, and they have been good and happy years. Susi's love, understanding, and support enriched my life immeasurably.

We started out with nothing, worked hard, and lived frugally, but never felt poor or deprived. My initial job keeping maintenance records for the L.A. Transit Lines' buses and streetcars made me take a class in bookkeeping at the local evening high school. It led to more advanced accounting studies at UCLA's evening classes over the next two years. During those early years we lived the typical new immigrants' life. Susi worked in a garment factory, had short careers as filing clerk, saleslady, and launderette attendant and finally as interior decorator. I survived one year of selling yardage in L.A.s biggest department store, and then worked as in-house accountant first at a coffee and spice factory, and then a financial company. After I passed the CPA (Certified Public Accountant) exam in 1952, we took an extended trip back to Europe. It was nice to visit old friends and family, but it also convinced us that the decision three years earlier to build a life in California was right.

Back in L.A. I started my career as a CPA first with one of the then big eight international accounting firms, and then in 1954 with Kenneth Leventhal in his three-man firm. The firm and Southern California grew rapidly. I became a partner in 1960. It was a demanding and challenging career. We were ambitious, capable, hardworking, and successful. The story of the firm of Kenneth Leventhal & Company is quite unique, but not the subject of this memoir. I was lucky to join it, and to be part of it. When I retired as a partner at the end of 1988, the firm had 1500 partners and employees, in 15 cities, and would soon be the ninth largest accounting firm in the country. I continued to work for the firm for another 10 years as a part time consultant, and assisted in the firm's 1995 merger with Ernst & Young.

Paul, Daniel, Gunilla, and Susanne, 1982

Susi's and my personal lives were immensely enriched by the birth of our son Daniel in 1954. We cherished the blessings and tribulations of parenthood, and were fortunate to share with him the years of his childhood, youth, and his adult life with Gunilla, Anya, and Shiri. All four added new meaning for us, and our life without their love would be empty and incomplete.

I could write many stories and details about our life over the last 60-plus years, but decided to end this memoir with the beginning of our life in California, a "normal" life as lived by normal people here and all over the Western world. What I tried to do was to describe the life of a child whose childhood at the age of six was interrupted by external events, and six years later shattered but eventually rebuilt and regained. My life was not unique; it reflects what happened to Jewish children in Europe born in the post-WWI years, most of whom by 1945 had been murdered. Nor is it unique among those who like me escaped and survived, most of whom successfully rebuilt their lives. But I will indulge in some reflections, reflections of a man in his 88th year, reflections on what was and still is a good life.

Susanne and Paul, summer 1949, California

REFLECTIONS AND OPINIONS

LUCK

I was lucky that my parents were willing to bring their children to safety, to part from them, not knowing how soon or if a reunion would be possible.

I was lucky to be put on a list to Sweden and not another European country later being occupied by the Germans.

I was lucky that Hitler lost the war, and thus assured my survival.

I was lucky to have good genes, good health, a good mind, and good looks.

FAMILY

A nice family makes for a good life. Acceptance of each other's personalities is a prerequisite. We cannot choose our relatives, but I would not have wanted to be without them, and I grieve for the many who were taken from us.

FRIENDS

We have made many friends, and they were very much part of our life. They enriched our existence. We miss too many already.

RELIGION

I have a strong sense of loyalty being a Jew and belonging to the Jewish people. I am not a believer in the Jewish religion's many rules and laws, but try to follow its ethical and moral concepts. We like to keep up some of its traditions and observe its holidays.

Paul Kester

I am very supportive of Jewish causes, both here and in Israel. Having witnessed the persecution and nearly successful extinction of European Jewry, I try to help pro-Jewish and pro-Israel institutions.

BIRTH

The birth of a child or a grandchild is a miracle. To have seen them grow and develop was part of life's highlights.

DEATH

It does not scare me, but it is difficult to imagine that in a relatively near future I will be dead, and no longer know what is happening, not to be part of the world.

MODERATION

I consider it a basic requirement in anybody's life. I tried to adhere to it, mostly with success.

FASHIONS AND TRENDS

I did not fight them, but felt never compelled to accept what I did not like or find worthwhile. By now I am quite happy to be "old-fashioned." Much of what nowadays is "in," I don't understand, and I don't miss it.

BOOKS AND MUSIC

I cannot imagine my life without them.

PHYSICAL ACTIVITY AND SPORTS

Regular exercise has kept me healthy and sane. Skiing was one of my best experiences, I loved it and did it until age 80, and still miss it.

MONEY

I was never consumed by it. Its importance to me was only that it is providing security and independence. And I enjoy the management of it.

POSSESSIONS

It was fun to acquire possessions, especially when we started with nothing. But I am not emotionally attached to "things," and I don't care what happens to "things" when I am gone.

CHARITY

Receiving: I readily accepted it when I needed it. I had no choice.
Giving: it gives me pleasure and satisfaction to be able to help others. We never acquired expensive tastes, but feel obligated to give back some of what we don't need.

GOODNESS AND HATE

Anne Frank in her diary wrote, *"in spite of everything I still believe that people are really good at heart."* I disagree. Too many people were or are still consciously seeking or exercising absolute power in the name of Nazism, Stalinism, militant Islam or other kinds of tribalism, or they are engaging in criminal and antisocial activities. They do not tolerate the lives of others, nor their lifestyles, ideas, religions, or possessions. I despise all intolerance.

ACCEPTANCE AND REGRETS

I could always accept what was beyond my ability to change, and I usually managed to see life in a positive light. I tried not to get upset by trivial nuisances, but to be optimistic, patient, and tolerant. I am happy to have lived in a free country and society, although I am sometimes annoyed by its messy disputes and small minds, but am glad that we all manage to live in peace.

I regret that the world was and still is full of strife, greed, envy, and poverty, but I hope that humanity will learn to create a better world for all.